Hot Lotto Numbers™

JEAN SIMPSON

Crown Publishers, Inc., New York

Also by Jean Simpson

Hot Numbers™
Shisha Mirror Embroidery

Copyright © 1987 by Jean Simpson

Published by Crown Publishers, Inc., 225 Park Avenue South, New York, New York 10003 and represented in Canada by the Canadian MANDA Group.

CROWN is a trademark of Crown Publishers, Inc.

HOT LOTTO NUMBERS, HOT NUMBERS, logos, and designs are trademarks of Jean Simpson

Manufactured in the United States of America

Library of Congress Cataloging-in-Publication Data

Simpson, Jean
  Hot lotto numbers.

  1. Lotto. I. Title.
GV1311.L6S46 1987   795.3   87-9130
ISBN 0-517-57072-6

10 9 8 7 6

CONTENTS

ACKNOWLEDGMENTS

Barbara Grossman, my brilliant editor and caring friend, whose energy and expertise guided this book.

Debbie Rubin, my creative publicist, for her dedication to my projects.

Kate Hammon, my accomplished assistant editor, whom I value for her efficiency and quick wit.

Libby Walker, my versatile assistant, who managed to smile as she asked, "The deadline is *when*?" and "*How* many charts?"

Michael Wallach, my personal manager extraordinaire, who encouraged me to write this book and who walked with me every step of the way.

Dennis Cohen, a mathematical genius, who developed the polynomial equations for the EXCHANGE CHART.

Roger Zissu, of Cowan, Liebowitz & Latman, my knowledgeable copyright and trademark attorney, for his expert legal advice.

Little did I think twenty years ago that my first visit to a numerologist would change the course of my life. What started out as a lark became an adventure that transformed me from a negative, insecure girl who was unable to communicate effectively with others, to the optimistic, confident woman I am today.

Eventually I decided to do what I loved most, and became a numerologist. As my clientele grew and my experience with it, I developed a philosophy: "Thoughts are things; whatever you can hold in your mind you can hold in your hand." Sharing that message became an important part of my numerology readings. The more I focused on the positive messages in my numbers, the more I seemed to attract positive people and experience positive events in my life. Seeing the good in myself helped me to see the good in others. It gave me great satisfaction when clients began to value my advice to live on the "hot" side of life almost as much as they counted on my interpretation of their numbers.

Gradually my reputation grew, and I was asked to deliver motivational talks. After one especially inspirational presentation, a full house of five hundred honored me with a standing ovation. It was a magical moment. That evening my telephone rang. It was a woman from the audience named Pat who was most complimentary, saying that my words touched her so much that she wanted to give *me* a gift—a personal reading. When she asked the date of my birth, I wondered if she were a numerologist or an astrologer. Pat told me that even though she was familiar with both sciences, her forte was a system based on playing cards. "Tell me your birthday and I'll tell you all about yourself," she said. I could hardly wait for our lunch date later that week.

During our meeting I was fascinated with the way Pat used her yearly card charts to relate information about my life. The jargon was familiar to me, and I knew the truth when I heard it: "Your card is in the Venus position in the Mars line. Be careful of arguments in your home this year." Suddenly Pat's words called to mind a century-old book given to me by my second numerology teacher: Olney Richmond's *The Magic of the Cards*. The book's formal, old-fashioned prose and complicated card system had overwhelmed me at first, so it had collected dust on my shelf ever since. Although I made progress, each time I attempted to unravel the mystery something always seemed to elude me.

Reminded once again of the cards, I was determined to renew my efforts until I could finally unlock the secrets of the ancient system. After months of studying, calculating, and memorizing, I mastered the material and began to incorporate my new-found knowledge into numerology readings for my clients. It became clear to me that the messages in the cards echoed the information in people's numbers.

had developed my own interpretation of numerology, I
that the cards could be transposed into numbers. I combined
gy, astrology, and cards to create a system that works every day
ear. I was able to predict with amazing accuracy, to the day,
of personal and business significance in the lives of my clients and
own life. My system withstood the test of time, proving itself
accurate year after year.

When clients began calling at 6 A.M. wanting to know what to expect
for the day, I questioned the wisdom of having shared my foolproof
system. Sometimes I regretted having developed it in the first place.
What had started out as a tool to help myself and a few others began to
fill my every waking moment, and a few sleeping ones as well.

That was a minor inconvenience compared to the deluge of requests I
received for ''lucky'' numbers when the lotto craze hit. I theorized that
my faithful daily system would work for lotto numbers as well.

People weren't satisfied knowing *one* group of lotto numbers; they
wanted several groups to play for every day of the week and variations to
fit every game in twenty-four states and several foreign countries. All I
had to do was use polynomial equations in order to make the numbers
work for all the different games.

So, almost in self-defense, I'm sharing my HOT LOTTO NUMBERS™
system with you in this book. The best of luck, and may all your numbers
be hot. I'll be looking for you in the winner's circle!

ABOUT THIS BOOK

If you know your birthday and can write the numbers from 1 to 52 and
the letters from A to Z, you can find your personal HOT LOTTO
NUMBERS for every day of the year.

HOW TO USE THE KEY NUMBER CHART

Like your birthday, your KEY NUMBER never changes. It has no
special meaning except as a first step to finding your HOT LOTTO
NUMBERS. You can find your KEY NUMBER on the chart below, in
the square where your birth *month* and birth *day* meet.

For example:

If your birthday is January 1, your KEY NUMBER is 52.

If your birthday is February 24, your KEY NUMBER is 27.

My birthday is August 23, so my KEY NUMBER is 16.

Now find *your* KEY NUMBER and write it down here. My KEY
NUMBER is __16__. *for Henry*

2 *u is 22 for Willard*

KEY NUMBER CHART

DAY	JAN.	FEB.	MAR.	APR.	MAY	JUNE	JULY	AUG.	SEPT.	OCT.	NOV.	DEC.
1	52	50	48	46	44	42	40	38	36	34	32	30
2	51	49	47	45	43	41	39	37	35	33	31	29
3	50	48	46	44	42	40	38	36	34	32	30	28
4	49	47	45	43	41	39	37	35	33	31	29	27
5	48	46	44	42	40	38	36	34	32	30	28	26
6	47	45	43	41	39	37	35	33	31	29	27	25
7	46	44	42	40	38	36	34	32	30	28	26	24
8	45	43	41	39	37	35	33	31	29	27	25	23
9	44	42	40	38	36	34	32	30	28	26	24	22
10	43	41	39	37	35	33	31	29	27	25	23	21
11	42	40	38	36	34	32	30	28	26	24	22	20
12	41	39	37	35	33	31	29	27	25	23	21	19
13	40	38	36	34	32	30	28	26	24	22	20	18
14	39	37	35	33	31	29	27	25	23	21	19	17
15	38	36	34	32	30	28	26	24	22	20	18	16
16	37	35	33	31	29	27	25	23	21	19	17	15
17	36	34	32	30	28	26	24	22	20	18	16	14
18	35	33	31	29	27	25	23	21	19	17	15	13
19	34	32	30	28	26	24	22	20	18	16	14	12
20	33	31	29	27	25	23	21	19	17	15	13	11
21	32	30	28	26	24	22	20	18	16	14	12	10
22	31	29	27	25	23	21	19	17	15	13	11	9
23	30	28	26	24	22	20	18	16	14	12	10	8
24	29	27	25	23	21	19	17	15	13	11	9	7
25	28	26	24	22	20	18	16	14	12	10	8	6
26	27	25	23	21	19	17	15	13	11	9	7	5
27	26	24	22	20	18	16	14	12	10	8	6	4
28	25	23	21	19	17	15	13	11	9	7	5	3
29	24	22	20	18	16	14	12	10	8	6	4	2
30	23		19	17	15	13	11	9	7	5	3	1
31	22		18		14		10	8		4		52

HOW TO FIND YOUR HOT LOTTO NUMBERS ON THE DAILY CHART

There are 365 DAILY CHARTS—one for each day of the year.
Each chart has 52 Balls, lettered from A to Z, AA to ZZ.
Here is a sample DAILY CHART.

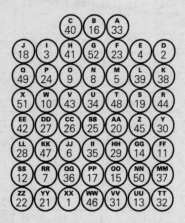

Let's use my KEY NUMBER 16 as an example.
Suppose I want to *buy* a lotto ticket on January 10. (Always use the DAILY CHART for the date you want to *buy* your lotto ticket.)
Find the KEY NUMBER 16 on the DAILY CHART for January 10.
KEY NUMBER 16 is in Ball U.

January 10

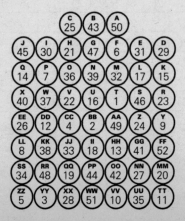

4

HOW TO USE THE PICK LISTS

Once you know the letter of the Ball on the DAILY CHART that contains your KEY NUMBER, you're ready to find the Balls that contain your HOT LOTTO NUMBERS.

There is a PICK LIST for every lotto game from PICK 1 to PICK 10.

Let's look at the PICK LIST for a PICK 6 lotto game on page 208. Notice that every Ball from A to ZZ is listed. Next to each Ball are three groups of letters. On the PICK LIST for PICK 6 each group has six letters. (On the PICK LIST for PICK 10 each group has ten letters, etc.) These letters tell you which Balls on the DAILY CHART contain your HOT LOTTO NUMBERS.

For example:

STEP 1　　Here is a section of the PICK LIST for PICK 6.
　　　　　　Find Ball U.

Ⓢ	T U V W X Y	L E UU NN GG Z	YY QQ II AA S K
Ⓣ	U V W X Y Z	M F A VV OO HH	ZZ RR JJ BB L D
Ⓤ	V W X Y Z AA	N G B WW PP II	SS KK CC U M E
Ⓥ	W X Y Z AA BB	O H C XX QQ JJ	LL DD V N F CC
Ⓦ	X Y Z AA BB CC	P I YY RR KK DD	LL EE W O G A

STEP 2　　I have copied the three groups of letters listed for Ball U below:

BALL	1ST GROUP	2ND GROUP	3RD GROUP
U	V W X Y Z AA	N G B WW PP II	SS KK CC U M E

5

STEP 3 Look again at the DAILY CHART for January 10.

January 10

You'll see that I've written the number corresponding to each letter below that letter. These are my HOT LOTTO NUMBERS for January 10.

BALL	1ST GROUP	2ND GROUP	3RD GROUP
U	V W X Y Z AA	N G B WW PP II	SS KK CC U M E
	22 37 40 9 24 49	39 47 43 51 44 18	34 38 4 16 32 31

Let's do another example:

Suppose I want to buy a PICK 4 lotto ticket on July 25, and my KEY NUMBER is 16.

STEP 1 Turn to the DAILY CHART for July 25.
Find KEY NUMBER 16.
It is in Ball B.

July 25

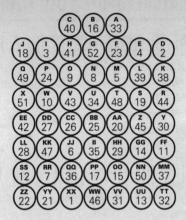

STEP 2   Since I'm playing a PICK 4 game, I need to use the PICK LIST
for PICK 4 on page 204. Here is a section of that list. Find
Ball B.

	1st col	2nd col	3rd col
Ⓐ	B C D E	VV OO HH AA	G O W EE
Ⓑ	C D E F	WW PP II BB	H P X F
Ⓒ	D E F G	XX QQ JJ CC	G M S Y

STEP 3   I have copied the three groups of letters listed for Ball B below:

BALL	1ST GROUP	2ND GROUP	3RD GROUP
B	C D E F	WW PP II BB	H P X F

STEP 4   Look again at the DAILY CHART for July 25. You'll see
that I've written the number corresponding to each letter below
that letter. These are my HOT LOTTO NUMBERS for July 25.

BALL	1ST GROUP	2ND GROUP	3RD GROUP
B	C D E F	WW PP II BB	H P X F
	40 2 4 23	46 17 35 25	41 24 51 23

HOW MANY TICKETS DO YOU WANT TO BUY?

IF YOU BUY ONE TO THREE TICKETS ON A GIVEN DAY If you
want to buy one ticket, use your first group of HOT LOTTO NUMBERS.

If you want to buy two tickets, use your first and second groups of
HOT LOTTO NUMBERS.

If you want to buy three tickets, use your first, second, and third
groups of HOT LOTTO NUMBERS.

IF YOU BUY FOUR OR MORE TICKETS ON A GIVEN DAY If
you're the last of the big-time spenders and you want to buy four or more
tickets on a given day, go back to the KEY NUMBER CHART on page
3.

Find another KEY NUMBER for a date other than your birthday. Let
your imagination run wild. Choose the birthday of someone close to you,
your wedding anniversary, or the date you fell in love.

Every KEY NUMBER you use will give you three groups of HOT
LOTTO NUMBERS—enough to buy three tickets.

HOW TO USE THE EXCHANGE CHART

WHY DO YOU NEED THE EXCHANGE CHART? Some lotto games
use the numbers 1–30, 1–36, 1–40, 1–42, 1–49, 1–56, 1–80, or 1–100.
But the HOT LOTTO NUMBERS system uses the numbers between 1
and 52.

Let's say your lotto game uses the numbers between 1 and 30, and
some of your HOT LOTTO NUMBERS are between 31 and 52. They
won't work in your 1–30 game. Relax, you can still use the HOT
LOTTO NUMBERS system by following the directions below.

WHAT IS THE EXCHANGE CHART? Look at the EXCHANGE
CHART on page 218. The numbers between 1 and 52 are listed in the left
column. Next to each number is a one-, two-, three-, or four-digit number
that you may use in exchange for your original HOT LOTTO NUMBER
1–52.

For example:

Let's say you want to play a 1–30 PICK 6 lotto game. Your first group of HOT LOTTO NUMBERS is 11, 38, 13, 52, 43, and 10.

The numbers 11, 13, and 10 *will* work in your 1–30 game, but 38, 52, and 43 are too high.

You need to use the EXCHANGE CHART to exchange 38, 52, and 43 for numbers between 1 and 30 to fit your game.

For example:

STEP 1   Turn to the EXCHANGE CHART on page 219. Find 38. The section of the EXCHANGE CHART for 38 is shown below.

38	1	98	168	2336

Exchange 38 for 1 because 1 will work in your 1–30 lotto game.

STEP 2   Find 52 on the EXCHANGE CHART on page 219. The section of the EXCHANGE CHART for 52 is shown below.

52	8	96	356	7324

Exchange 52 for 8 because 8 will work in your 1–30 lotto game.

STEP 3   Find 43 on the EXCHANGE CHART on page 219. The section of the EXCHANGE CHART for 43 is shown below.

43	2	14	179	3941

Exchange 43 for 2 because 2 works in your 1–30 lotto game. Why use 2 when 14 will work also? Because 2 is the first number in the row that works in your 1–30 game. If 2 were already one of your HOT LOTTO NUMBERS, you could use 14 because it also works in your 1–30 game.

WHAT DO YOU DO IF THE EXCHANGED NUMBER IS THE SAME AS ANOTHER ONE OF YOUR HOT LOTTO NUMBERS?

For example, let's say your PICK 6 lotto game uses numbers between 1 and 40. Suppose your HOT LOTTO NUMBERS are 5, 15, 47, 23, 18, and 20.

The only number that is too high for your 1–40 lotto game is 47.

Look at the EXCHANGE CHART on page 219. Find 47. The section of the EXCHANGE CHART for 47 is shown below.

47	5	87	742	1784

The only number you can exchange for 47 that will work in your 1–40 lotto game is 5. But 5 is already in your first group of HOT LOTTO NUMBERS. You can't use 5 twice on one ticket. What should you do? Don't play that group of HOT LOTTO NUMBERS. Go on to your second or third group if necessary.

WHAT DO YOU DO IF YOU CAN'T USE ANY OF YOUR THREE GROUPS OF HOT LOTTO NUMBERS BECAUSE OF DUPLICATE NUMBERS?

The chances of the sky falling are greater than your having duplicate numbers in all three groups. If none of your exchanged numbers works, save your money and play lotto another day.

If you're determined to tempt fate, use a KEY NUMBER from a date other than your birthday. Find the HOT LOTTO NUMBERS for the new KEY NUMBER. By the way, say hello to Chicken Little for me on your way to buy your lotto ticket. And good luck!

HOW DO YOU PLAY A 1–100 GAME?

The HOT LOTTO NUMBERS system uses numbers between 1 and 52. You may play your HOT LOTTO NUMBERS as is, or you may use the EXCHANGE CHART to exchange any of your HOT LOTTO NUMBERS for numbers between 53 and 100.

DO YOU NEED A TWO-, THREE-, OR FOUR-DIGIT NUMBER FOR YOUR PICK 1 LOTTO GAME?

Use the PICK LIST for a PICK 1 game.

If your HOT LOTTO NUMBER is a single digit, exchange it for the two-, three-, or four-digit number your game requires, using the EX-CHANGE CHART on page 218.

For example, let's say you need a two-, three- or four-digit number and your HOT LOTTO NUMBER is 5. Look at 5 on the EXCHANGE CHART on page 218. The section of the EXCHANGE CHART for 5 is shown below.

5		1	35	780	4225

If you need a two-digit number, exchange 5 for 35.

If you need a three-digit number, exchange 5 for 780.

If you need a four-digit number, exchange 5 for 4225.

If your HOT LOTTO NUMBER is a two-digit number, use the EX-CHANGE CHART on page 218 to exchange it for the three- or four-digit number your game requires.

For example, let's say you need a three- or four-digit number for your lotto game and your HOT LOTTO NUMBER is 32.

Look at the EXCHANGE CHART. Find 32. The section of the EX-CHANGE CHART for 32 is shown below.

32		6	64	192	5040

If you need a three-digit number, exchange 32 for 192.

If you need a four-digit number, exchange 32 for 5040.

DO YOU NEED A THREE-DIGIT NUMBER IN WHICH TWO DIGITS ARE THE SAME FOR A PICK 1 GAME? Use the PICK LIST for a PICK 1 game.

If your HOT LOTTO NUMBER is a single digit, use the EXCHANGE CHART on page 218 to exchange your single-digit number for a two-digit number.

For example, let's say your HOT LOTTO NUMBER is 4. Find 4 on the EXCHANGE CHART on page 218. The section of the EXCHANGE CHART for 4 is shown below.

4		4	48	692	8896

Exchange 4 for 48. *Repeat the last digit,* giving you the three-digit number, 488.

If you need a three-digit number in which the first two digits are the same, *repeat the first digit,* giving you 448.

If your HOT LOTTO NUMBER is a two-digit number, repeat one of the digits to make a three-digit number.

For example, let's say your HOT LOTTO NUMBER is 28. Repeat the *last digit,* giving you 288. Or, if you need a three-digit number in which the first two digits are the same, *repeat the first digit,* giving you 228.

HOW TO USE WHAT YOU HAVE LEARNED

You know how to find your HOT LOTTO NUMBERS and how to use them in different lotto games. Let's review the steps.

1. Find your KEY NUMBER on the KEY NUMBER CHART on page 3.

2. Turn to the DAILY CHART for the day you're going to *buy* a lotto ticket.

3. Find your KEY NUMBER in a Ball on the DAILY CHART.

4. Turn to the PICK LIST (PICK 1–PICK 10) appropriate to your game.

5. On the PICK LIST, find the letter of the Ball that contains your KEY NUMBER.

6. Write down the three groups of letters.

7. Look again at the DAILY CHART for the day you want to *buy* a lotto ticket. Below each letter on your list, write the number that is in that Ball.

8. Use the HOT LOTTO NUMBERS for the first, second, and third groups in order, depending on how many tickets you want to buy.

9. Use the EXCHANGE CHART on page 218 if needed for numbers that fit your game.

365 DAILY CHARTS

JANUARY 1

NOTES

		C 18	B 52	A 43		
J 28	I 51	H 19	G 4	F 34	E 14	D 24
Q 9	P 39	O 25	N 33	M 15	L 50	K 10
X 35	W 21	V 47	U 11	T 44	S 29	R 12
EE 20	DD 5	CC 49	BB 45	AA 30	Z 8	Y 40
LL 6	KK 31	JJ 16	II 1	HH 7	GG 36	FF 26
SS 32	RR 17	QQ 2	PP 27	OO 37	NN 22	MM 3
ZZ 38	YY 46	XX 23	WW 13	VV 41	UU 48	TT 42

JANUARY 2

NOTES

		C 5	B 51	A 30		
J 15	I 50	H 6	G 35	F 21	E 1	D 11
Q 44	P 26	O 12	N 20	M 2	L 49	K 45
X 22	W 8	V 40	U 46	T 31	S 16	R 41
EE 7	DD 36	CC 48	BB 32	AA 17	Z 42	Y 27
LL 37	KK 18	JJ 3	II 38	HH 52	GG 23	FF 13
SS 19	RR 4	QQ 34	PP 14	OO 24	NN 9	MM 39
ZZ 25	YY 33	XX 10	WW 43	VV 28	UU 47	TT 29

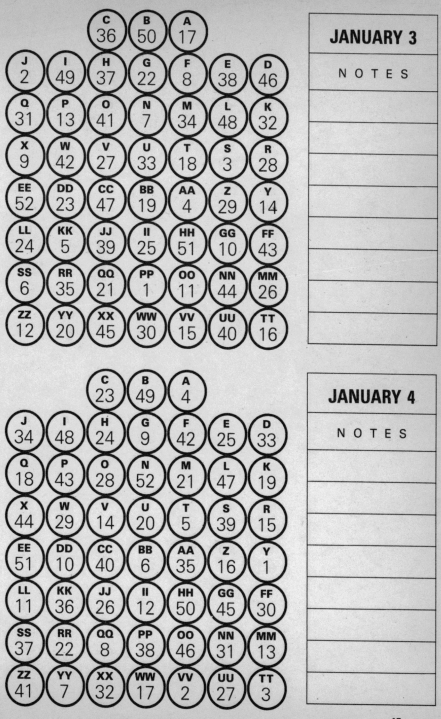

JANUARY 3

NOTES

JANUARY 4

NOTES

15

JANUARY 5

NOTES

		C 10	B 48	A 35		
J 21	I 47	H 11	G 44	F 29	E 12	D 20
Q 5	P 30	O 15	N 51	M 8	L 40	K 6
X 31	W 16	V 1	U 7	T 36	S 26	R 2
EE 50	DD 45	CC 27	BB 37	AA 22	Z 3	Y 38
LL 46	KK 23	JJ 13	II 41	HH 49	GG 32	FF 17
SS 24	RR 9	QQ 42	PP 25	OO 33	NN 18	MM 43
ZZ 28	YY 52	XX 19	WW 4	VV 34	UU 14	TT 39

JANUARY 6

NOTES

		C 45	B 47	A 22		
J 8	I 40	H 46	G 31	F 16	E 41	D 7
Q 36	P 17	O 2	N 50	M 42	L 27	K 37
X 18	W 3	V 38	U 52	T 23	S 13	R 34
EE 49	DD 32	CC 14	BB 24	AA 9	Z 39	Y 25
LL 33	KK 10	JJ 43	II 28	HH 48	GG 19	FF 4
SS 11	RR 44	QQ 29	PP 12	OO 20	NN 5	MM 30
ZZ 15	YY 51	XX 6	WW 35	VV 21	UU 1	TT 26

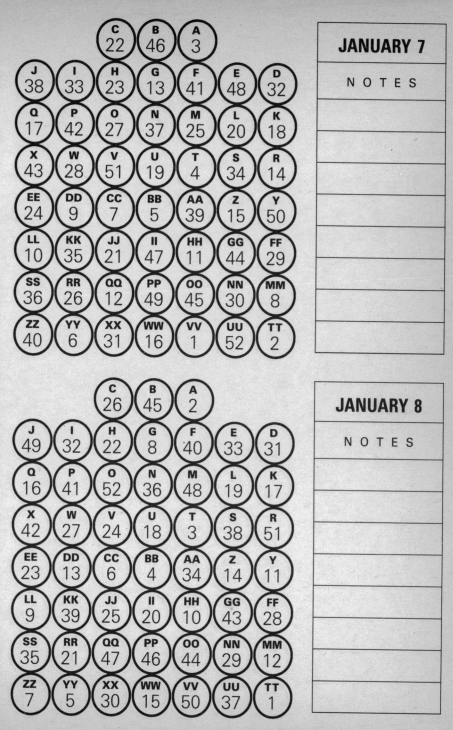

JANUARY 7

NOTES

JANUARY 8

NOTES

JANUARY 9

NOTES

C 21 B 44 A 1

J 46 I 31 H 26 G 12 F 7 E 32 D 30

Q 15 P 40 O 37 N 35 M 33 L 18 K 16

X 41 W 52 V 23 U 17 T 2 S 49 R 24

EE 22 DD 8 CC 5 BB 3 AA 38 Z 51 Y 10

LL 13 KK 34 JJ 48 II 19 HH 9 GG 42 FF 27

SS 39 RR 25 QQ 20 PP 45 OO 43 NN 28 MM 47

ZZ 6 YY 4 XX 29 WW 14 VV 11 UU 36 TT 50

JANUARY 10

NOTES

C 25 B 43 A 50

J 45 I 30 H 21 G 47 F 6 E 31 D 29

Q 14 P 7 O 36 N 39 M 32 L 17 K 15

X 40 W 37 V 22 U 16 T 1 S 46 R 23

EE 26 DD 12 CC 4 BB 2 AA 49 Z 24 Y 9

LL 8 KK 38 JJ 33 II 18 HH 13 GG 41 FF 52

SS 34 RR 48 QQ 19 PP 44 OO 42 NN 27 MM 20

ZZ 5 YY 3 XX 28 WW 51 VV 10 UU 35 TT 11

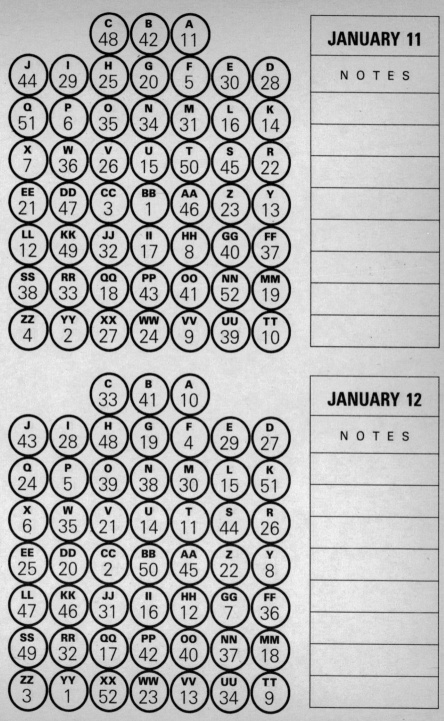

JANUARY 11

NOTES

JANUARY 12

NOTES

JANUARY 13

N O T E S

C 32	B 40	A 9

J 42	I 27	H 33	G 18	F 3	E 28	D 52
Q 23	P 4	O 34	N 49	M 29	L 14	K 24
X 5	W 39	V 25	U 51	T 10	S 43	R 21
EE 48	DD 19	CC 1	BB 11	AA 44	Z 26	Y 12
LL 20	KK 45	JJ 30	II 15	HH 47	GG 6	FF 35
SS 46	RR 31	QQ 16	PP 41	OO 7	NN 36	MM 17
ZZ 2	YY 50	XX 37	WW 22	VV 8	UU 38	TT 13

JANUARY 14

N O T E S

C 14	B 39	A 7

J 36	I 26	H 15	G 50	F 45	E 22	D 21
Q 47	P 46	O 31	N 29	M 23	L 13	K 12
X 49	W 32	V 17	U 8	T 40	S 37	R 18
EE 16	DD 1	CC 43	BB 41	AA 52	Z 19	Y 4
LL 2	KK 27	JJ 24	II 9	HH 3	GG 38	FF 33
SS 28	RR 51	QQ 10	PP 35	OO 34	NN 48	MM 11
ZZ 44	YY 42	XX 25	WW 20	VV 5	UU 30	TT 6

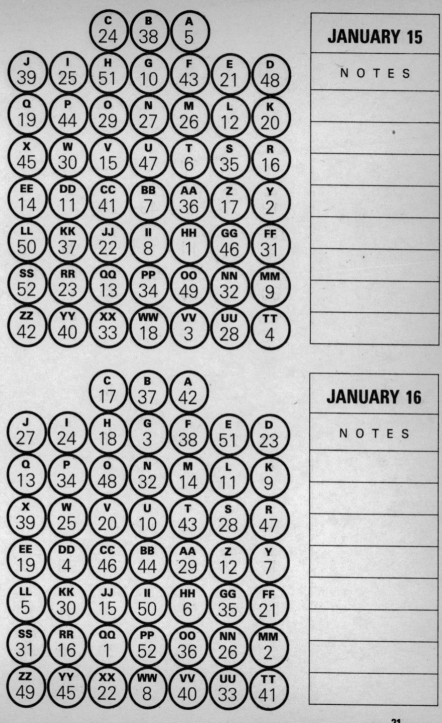

JANUARY 15

NOTES

JANUARY 16

NOTES

21

JANUARY 17

NOTES

		C 16	B 36	A 41		
J 52	I 23	H 17	G 2	F 49	E 24	D 22
Q 8	P 38	O 33	N 31	M 51	L 10	K 13
X 34	W 48	V 19	U 9	T 42	S 27	R 20
EE 18	DD 3	CC 45	BB 43	AA 28	Z 47	Y 6
LL 4	KK 29	JJ 14	II 11	HH 5	GG 39	FF 25
SS 30	RR 15	QQ 50	PP 37	OO 35	NN 21	MM 1
ZZ 46	YY 44	XX 26	WW 12	VV 7	UU 32	TT 40

JANUARY 18

NOTES

		C 15	B 35	A 40		
J 37	I 22	H 16	G 1	F 46	E 23	D 26
Q 12	P 49	O 32	N 30	M 24	L 9	K 8
X 38	W 33	V 18	U 13	T 41	S 52	R 19
EE 17	DD 2	CC 44	BB 42	AA 27	Z 20	Y 5
LL 3	KK 28	JJ 51	II 10	HH 4	GG 34	FF 48
SS 29	RR 14	QQ 11	PP 36	OO 39	NN 25	MM 50
ZZ 45	YY 43	XX 21	WW 47	VV 6	UU 31	TT 7

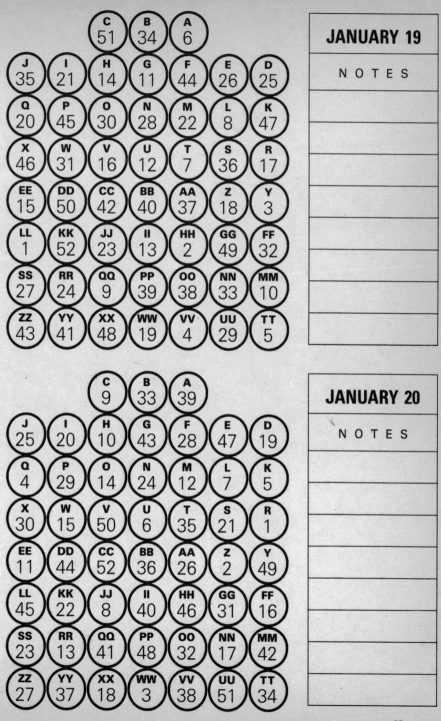

JANUARY 19

NOTES

JANUARY 20

NOTES

23

JANUARY 21

NOTES

		C 13	B 32	A 34		
J 48	I 19	H 9	G 42	F 27	E 20	D 18
Q 3	P 28	O 51	N 23	M 47	L 6	K 4
X 29	W 14	V 11	U 5	T 39	S 25	R 50
EE 10	DD 43	CC 37	BB 35	AA 21	Z 1	Y 46
LL 44	KK 26	JJ 12	II 7	HH 45	GG 30	FF 15
SS 22	RR 8	QQ 40	PP 33	OO 31	NN 16	MM 41
ZZ 52	YY 36	XX 17	WW 2	VV 49	UU 24	TT 38

JANUARY 22

NOTES

		C 8	B 31	A 38		
J 33	I 18	H 13	G 41	F 52	E 19	D 17
Q 2	P 27	O 24	N 22	M 20	L 5	K 3
X 28	W 51	V 10	U 4	T 34	S 48	R 11
EE 9	DD 42	CC 36	BB 39	AA 25	Z 50	Y 45
LL 43	KK 21	JJ 47	II 6	HH 44	GG 29	FF 14
SS 26	RR 12	QQ 7	PP 32	OO 30	NN 15	MM 40
ZZ 37	YY 35	XX 16	WW 1	VV 46	UU 23	TT 49

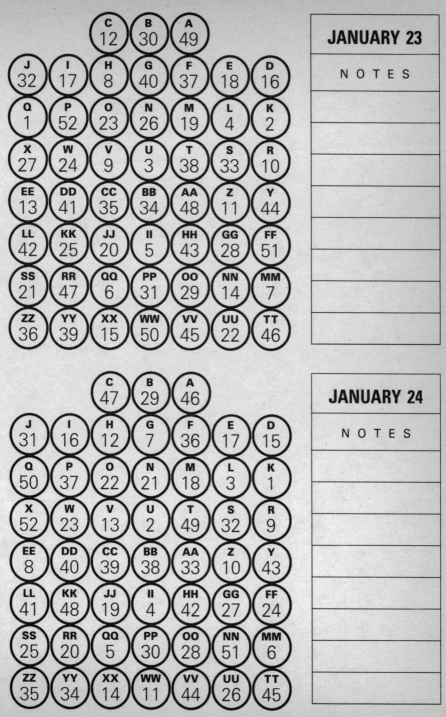

JANUARY 23

NOTES

JANUARY 24

NOTES

25

JANUARY 25

NOTES

C 20 · B 28 · A 45

J 30 · I 15 · H 47 · G 6 · F 35 · E 16 · D 14

Q 11 · P 36 · O 26 · N 25 · M 17 · L 2 · K 50

X 37 · W 22 · V 8 · U 1 · T 46 · S 31 · R 13

EE 12 · DD 7 · CC 34 · BB 49 · AA 32 · Z 9 · Y 42

LL 40 · KK 33 · JJ 18 · II 3 · HH 41 · GG 52 · FF 23

SS 48 · RR 19 · QQ 4 · PP 29 · OO 27 · NN 24 · MM 5

ZZ 39 · YY 38 · XX 51 · WW 10 · VV 43 · UU 21 · TT 44

JANUARY 26

NOTES

C 19 · B 27 · A 44

J 29 · I 14 · H 20 · G 5 · F 39 · E 15 · D 51

Q 10 · P 35 · O 21 · N 48 · M 16 · L 1 · K 11

X 36 · W 26 · V 12 · U 50 · T 45 · S 30 · R 8

EE 47 · DD 6 · CC 38 · BB 46 · AA 31 · Z 13 · Y 41

LL 7 · KK 32 · JJ 17 · II 2 · HH 40 · GG 37 · FF 22

SS 33 · RR 18 · QQ 3 · PP 28 · OO 52 · NN 23 · MM 4

ZZ 34 · YY 49 · XX 24 · WW 9 · VV 42 · UU 25 · TT 43

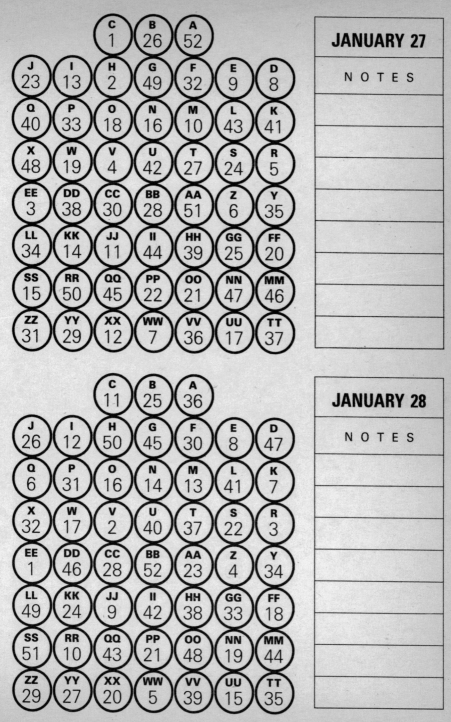

JANUARY 27

NOTES

JANUARY 28

NOTES

JANUARY 29

NOTES

		C 4	B 24	A 29		
J 14	I 11	H 5	G 39	F 25	E 50	D 10
Q 43	P 21	O 47	N 19	M 1	L 46	K 44
X 26	W 12	V 7	U 45	T 30	S 15	R 40
EE 6	DD 35	CC 33	BB 31	AA 16	Z 41	Y 52
LL 36	KK 17	JJ 2	II 49	HH 37	GG 22	FF 8
SS 18	RR 3	QQ 38	PP 51	OO 23	NN 13	MM 34
ZZ 48	YY 32	XX 9	WW 42	VV 27	UU 20	TT 28

JANUARY 30

NOTES

		C 3	B 23	A 28		
J 51	I 10	H 4	G 34	F 48	E 11	D 9
Q 42	P 25	O 20	N 18	M 50	L 45	K 43
X 21	W 47	V 6	U 44	T 29	S 14	R 7
EE 5	DD 39	CC 32	BB 30	AA 15	Z 40	Y 37
LL 35	KK 16	JJ 1	II 46	HH 36	GG 26	FF 12
SS 17	RR 2	QQ 49	PP 24	OO 22	NN 8	MM 38
ZZ 33	YY 31	XX 13	WW 41	VV 52	UU 19	TT 27

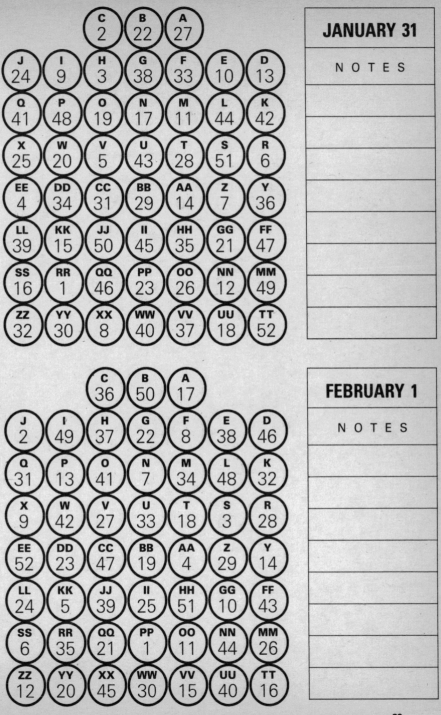

FEBRUARY 2

NOTES

		C 23	B 49	A 4		
J 34	I 48	H 24	G 9	F 42	E 25	D 33
Q 18	P 43	O 28	N 52	M 21	L 47	K 19
X 44	W 29	V 14	U 20	T 5	S 39	R 15
EE 51	DD 10	CC 40	BB 6	AA 35	Z 16	Y 1
LL 11	KK 36	JJ 26	II 12	HH 50	GG 45	FF 30
SS 37	RR 22	QQ 8	PP 38	OO 46	NN 31	MM 13
ZZ 41	YY 7	XX 32	WW 17	VV 2	UU 27	TT 3

FEBRUARY 3

NOTES

		C 10	B 48	A 35		
J 21	I 47	H 11	G 44	F 29	E 12	D 20
Q 5	P 30	O 15	N 51	M 8	L 40	K 6
X 31	W 16	V 1	U 7	T 36	S 26	R 2
EE 50	DD 45	CC 27	BB 37	AA 22	Z 3	Y 38
LL 46	KK 23	JJ 13	II 41	HH 49	GG 32	FF 17
SS 24	RR 9	QQ 42	PP 25	OO 33	NN 18	MM 43
ZZ 28	YY 52	XX 19	WW 4	VV 34	UU 14	TT 39

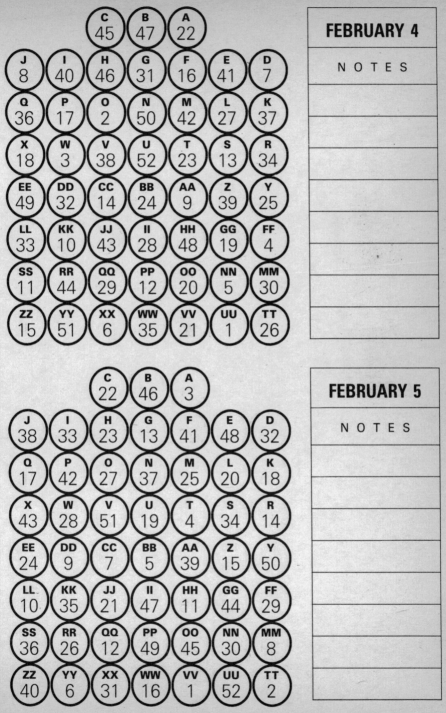

FEBRUARY 4

NOTES

FEBRUARY 5

NOTES

31

FEBRUARY 6

NOTES

C 26	B 45	A 2	
J 49	I 32	H 22	G 8	F 40	E 33	D 31
Q 16	P 41	O 52	N 36	M 48	L 19	K 17
X 42	W 27	V 24	U 18	T 3	S 38	R 51
EE 23	DD 13	CC 6	BB 4	AA 34	Z 14	Y 11
LL 9	KK 39	JJ 25	II 20	HH 10	GG 43	FF 28
SS 35	RR 21	QQ 47	PP 46	OO 44	NN 29	MM 12
ZZ 7	YY 5	XX 30	WW 15	VV 50	UU 37	TT 1

FEBRUARY 7

NOTES

C 21	B 44	A 1	
J 46	I 31	H 26	G 12	F 7	E 32	D 30
Q 15	P 40	O 37	N 35	M 33	L 18	K 16
X 41	W 52	V 23	U 17	T 2	S 49	R 24
EE 22	DD 8	CC 5	BB 3	AA 38	Z 51	Y 10
LL 13	KK 34	JJ 48	II 19	HH 9	GG 42	FF 27
SS 39	RR 25	QQ 20	PP 45	OO 43	NN 28	MM 47
ZZ 6	YY 4	XX 29	WW 14	VV 11	UU 36	TT 50

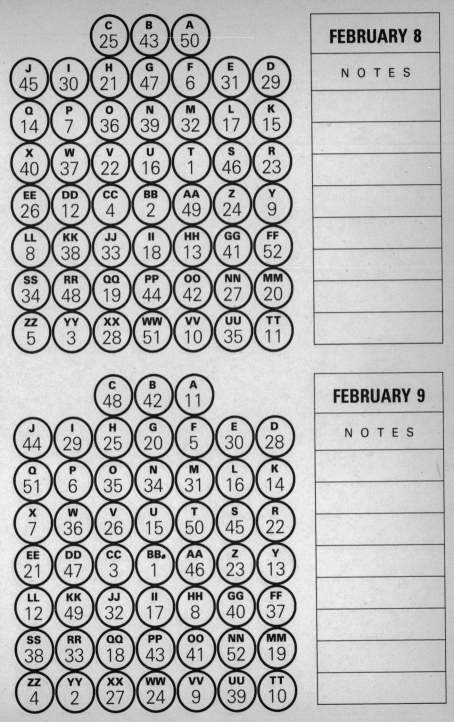

FEBRUARY 10

NOTES

C 33 · B 41 · A 10
J 43 · I 28 · H 48 · G 19 · F 4 · E 29 · D 27
Q 24 · P 5 · O 39 · N 38 · M 30 · L 15 · K 51
X 6 · W 35 · V 21 · U 14 · T 11 · S 44 · R 26
EE 25 · DD 20 · CC 2 · BB 50 · AA 45 · Z 22 · Y 8
LL 47 · KK 46 · JJ 31 · II 16 · HH 12 · GG 7 · FF 36
SS 49 · RR 32 · QQ 17 · PP 42 · OO 40 · NN 37 · MM 18
ZZ 3 · YY 1 · XX 52 · WW 23 · VV 13 · UU 34 · TT 9

FEBRUARY 11

NOTES

C 32 · B 40 · A 9
J 42 · I 27 · H 33 · G 18 · F 3 · E 28 · D 52
Q 23 · P 4 · O 34 · N 49 · M 29 · L 14 · K 24
X 5 · W 39 · V 25 · U 51 · T 10 · S 43 · R 21
EE 48 · DD 19 · CC 1 · BB 11 · AA 44 · Z 26 · Y 12
LL 20 · KK 45 · JJ 30 · II 15 · HH 47 · GG 6 · FF 35
SS 46 · RR 31 · QQ 16 · PP 41 · OO 7 · NN 36 · MM 17
ZZ 2 · YY 50 · XX 37 · WW 22 · VV 8 · UU 38 · TT 13

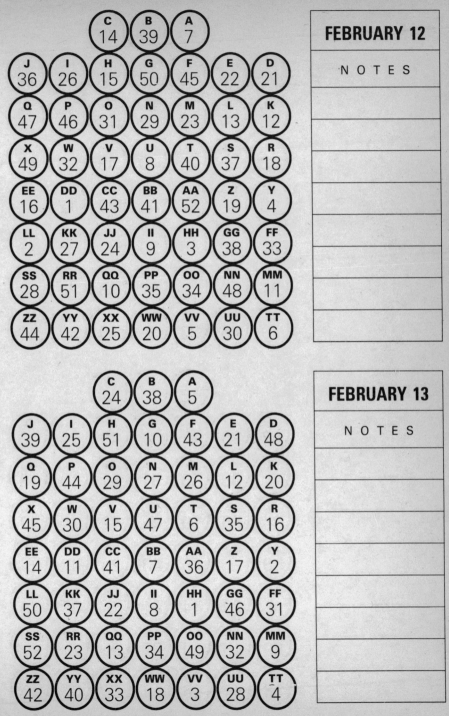

FEBRUARY 14

NOTES

C 17　B 37　A 42

J 27　I 24　H 18　G 3　F 38　E 51　D 23

Q 13　P 34　O 48　N 32　M 14　L 11　K 9

X 39　W 25　V 20　U 10　T 43　S 28　R 47

EE 19　DD 4　CC 46　BB 44　AA 29　Z 12　Y 7

LL 5　KK 30　JJ 15　II 50　HH 6　GG 35　FF 21

SS 31　RR 16　QQ 1　PP 52　OO 36　NN 26　MM 2

ZZ 49　YY 45　XX 22　WW 8　VV 40　UU 33　TT 41

FEBRUARY 15

NOTES

C 16　B 36　A 41

J 52　I 23　H 17　G 2　F 49　E 24　D 22

Q 8　P 38　O 33　N 31　M 51　L 10　K 13

X 34　W 48　V 19　U 9　T 42　S 27　R 20

EE 18　DD 3　CC 45　BB 43　AA 28　Z 47　Y 6

LL 4　KK 29　JJ 14　II 11　HH 5　GG 39　FF 25

SS 30　RR 15　QQ 50　PP 37　OO 35　NN 21　MM 1

ZZ 46　YY 44　XX 26　WW 12　VV 7　UU 32　TT 40

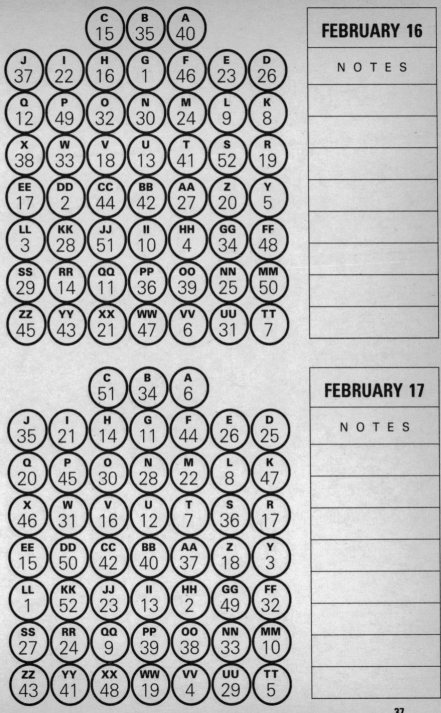

FEBRUARY 18

NOTES

C 9, B 33, A 39

J 25, I 20, H 10, G 43, F 28, E 47, D 19

Q 4, P 29, O 14, N 24, M 12, L 7, K 5

X 30, W 15, V 50, U 6, T 35, S 21, R 1

EE 11, DD 44, CC 52, BB 36, AA 26, Z 2, Y 49

LL 45, KK 22, JJ 8, II 40, HH 46, GG 31, FF 16

SS 23, RR 13, QQ 41, PP 48, OO 32, NN 17, MM 42

ZZ 27, YY 37, XX 18, WW 3, VV 38, UU 51, TT 34

FEBRUARY 19

NOTES

C 13, B 32, A 34

J 48, I 19, H 9, G 42, F 27, E 20, D 18

Q 3, P 28, O 51, N 23, M 47, L 6, K 4

X 29, W 14, V 11, U 5, T 39, S 25, R 50

EE 10, DD 43, CC 37, BB 35, AA 21, Z 1, Y 46

LL 44, KK 26, JJ 12, II 7, HH 45, GG 30, FF 15

SS 22, RR 8, QQ 40, PP 33, OO 31, NN 16, MM 41

ZZ 52, YY 36, XX 17, WW 2, VV 49, UU 24, TT 38

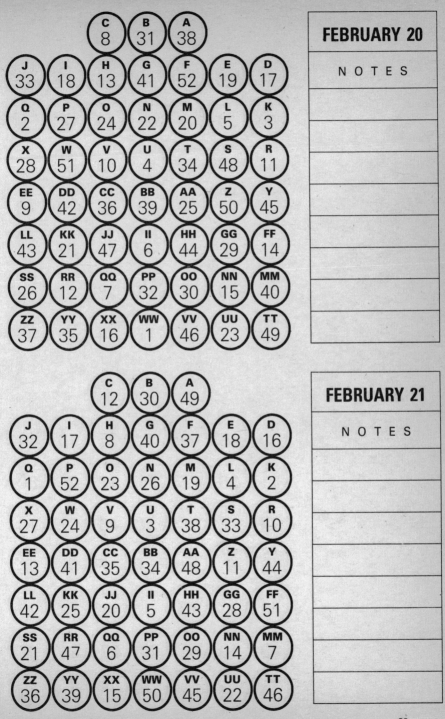

FEBRUARY 20

NOTES

FEBRUARY 21

NOTES

39

FEBRUARY 22

NOTES

		C 47	B 29	A 46		
J 31	I 16	H 12	G 7	F 36	E 17	D 15
Q 50	P 37	O 22	N 21	M 18	L 3	K 1
X 52	W 23	V 13	U 2	T 49	S 32	R 9
EE 8	DD 40	CC 39	BB 38	AA 33	Z 10	Y 43
LL 41	KK 48	JJ 19	II 4	HH 42	GG 27	FF 24
SS 25	RR 20	QQ 5	PP 30	OO 28	NN 51	MM 6
ZZ 35	YY 34	XX 14	WW 11	VV 44	UU 26	TT 45

FEBRUARY 23

NOTES

		C 20	B 28	A 45		
J 30	I 15	H 47	G 6	F 35	E 16	D 14
Q 11	P 36	O 26	N 25	M 17	L 2	K 50
X 37	W 22	V 8	U 1	T 46	S 31	R 13
EE 12	DD 7	CC 34	BB 49	AA 32	Z 9	Y 42
LL 40	KK 33	JJ 18	II 3	HH 41	GG 52	FF 23
SS 48	RR 19	QQ 4	PP 29	OO 27	NN 24	MM 5
ZZ 39	YY 38	XX 51	WW 10	VV 43	UU 21	TT 44

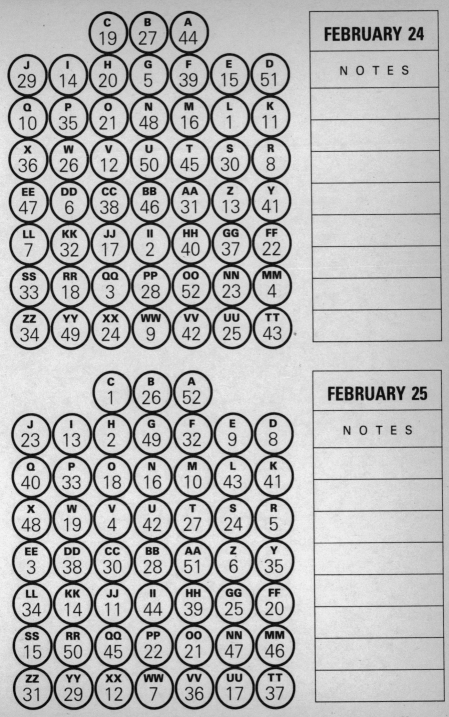

FEBRUARY 24

NOTES

FEBRUARY 25

NOTES

41

FEBRUARY 26

NOTES

C 11   B 25   A 36

J 26   I 12   H 50   G 45   F 30   E 8   D 47

Q 6   P 31   O 16   N 14   M 13   L 41   K 7

X 32   W 17   V 2   U 40   T 37   S 22   R 3

EE 1   DD 46   CC 28   BB 52   AA 23   Z 4   Y 34

LL 49   KK 24   JJ 9   II 42   HH 38   GG 33   FF 18

SS 51   RR 10   QQ 43   PP 21   OO 48   NN 19   MM 44

ZZ 29   YY 27   XX 20   WW 5   VV 39   UU 15   TT 35

FEBRUARY 27

NOTES

C 4   B 24   A 29

J 14   I 11   H 5   G 39   F 25   E 50   D 10

Q 43   P 21   O 47   N 19   M 1   L 46   K 44

X 26   W 12   V 7   U 45   T 30   S 15   R 40

EE 6   DD 35   CC 33   BB 31   AA 16   Z 41   Y 52

LL 36   KK 17   JJ 2   II 49   HH 37   GG 22   FF 8

SS 18   RR 3   QQ 38   PP 51   OO 23   NN 13   MM 34

ZZ 48   YY 32   XX 9   WW 42   VV 27   UU 20   TT 28

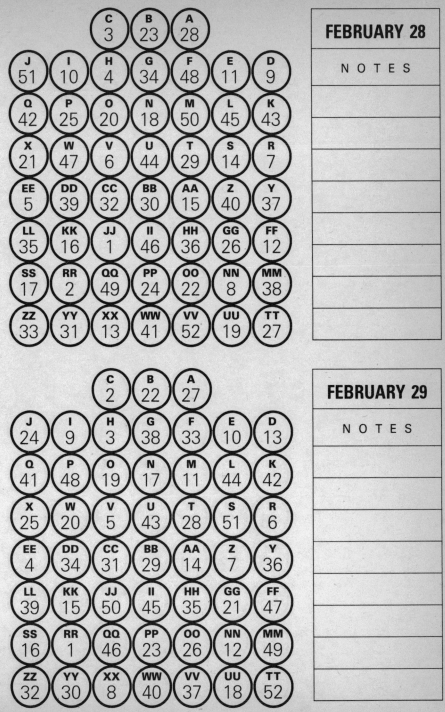

FEBRUARY 28

NOTES

FEBRUARY 29

NOTES

MARCH 1

NOTES

		C 10	B 48	A 35		
J 21	I 47	H 11	G 44	F 29	E 12	D 20
Q 5	P 30	O 15	N 51	M 8	L 40	K 6
X 31	W 16	V 1	U 7	T 36	S 26	R 2
EE 50	DD 45	CC 27	BB 37	AA 22	Z 3	Y 38
LL 46	KK 23	JJ 13	II 41	HH 49	GG 32	FF 17
SS 24	RR 9	QQ 42	PP 25	OO 33	NN 18	MM 43
ZZ 28	YY 52	XX 19	WW 4	VV 34	UU 14	TT 39

MARCH 2

NOTES

		C 45	B 47	A 22		
J 8	I 40	H 46	G 31	F 16	E 41	D 7
Q 36	P 17	O 2	N 50	M 42	L 27	K 37
X 18	W 3	V 38	U 52	T 23	S 13	R 34
EE 49	DD 32	CC 14	BB 24	AA 9	Z 39	Y 25
LL 33	KK 10	JJ 43	II 28	HH 48	GG 19	FF 4
SS 11	RR 44	QQ 29	PP 12	OO 20	NN 5	MM 30
ZZ 15	YY 51	XX 6	WW 35	VV 21	UU 1	TT 26

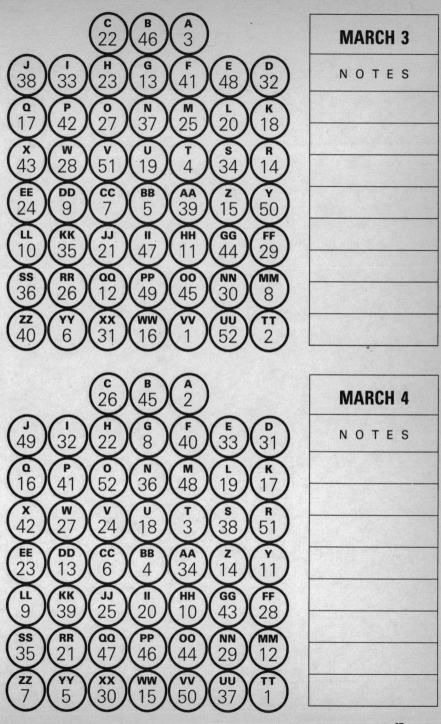

MARCH 3

NOTES

MARCH 4

NOTES

45

MARCH 5

NOTES

C 21	B 44	A 1				
J 46	I 31	H 26	G 12	F 7	E 32	D 30
Q 15	P 40	O 37	N 35	M 33	L 18	K 16
X 41	W 52	V 23	U 17	T 2	S 49	R 24
EE 22	DD 8	CC 5	BB 3	AA 38	Z 51	Y 10
LL 13	KK 34	JJ 48	II 19	HH 9	GG 42	FF 27
SS 39	RR 25	QQ 20	PP 45	OO 43	NN 28	MM 47
ZZ 6	YY 4	XX 29	WW 14	VV 11	UU 36	TT 50

MARCH 6

NOTES

C 25	B 43	A 50				
J 45	I 30	H 21	G 47	F 6	E 31	D 29
Q 14	P 7	O 36	N 39	M 32	L 17	K 15
X 40	W 37	V 22	U 16	T 1	S 46	R 23
EE 26	DD 12	CC 4	BB 2	AA 49	Z 24	Y 9
LL 8	KK 38	JJ 33	II 18	HH 13	GG 41	FF 52
SS 34	RR 48	QQ 19	PP 44	OO 42	NN 27	MM 20
ZZ 5	YY 3	XX 28	WW 51	VV 10	UU 35	TT 11

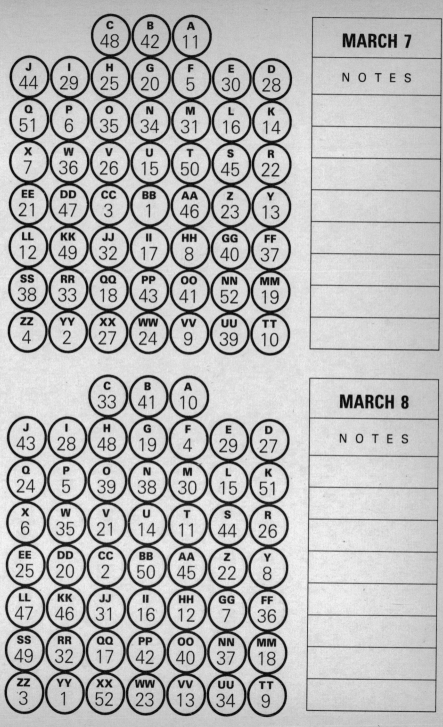

MARCH 7

NOTES

MARCH 8

NOTES

47

MARCH 9

NOTES

C 32, B 40, A 9

J 42, I 27, H 33, G 18, F 3, E 28, D 52

Q 23, P 4, O 34, N 49, M 29, L 14, K 24

X 5, W 39, V 25, U 51, T 10, S 43, R 21

EE 48, DD 19, CC 1, BB 11, AA 44, Z 26, Y 12

LL 20, KK 45, JJ 30, II 15, HH 47, GG 6, FF 35

SS 46, RR 31, QQ 16, PP 41, OO 7, NN 36, MM 17

ZZ 2, YY 50, XX 37, WW 22, VV 8, UU 38, TT 13

MARCH 10

NOTES

C 14, B 39, A 7

J 36, I 26, H 15, G 50, F 45, E 22, D 21

Q 47, P 46, O 31, N 29, M 23, L 13, K 12

X 49, W 32, V 17, U 8, T 40, S 37, R 18

EE 16, DD 1, CC 43, BB 41, AA 52, Z 19, Y 4

LL 2, KK 27, JJ 24, II 9, HH 3, GG 38, FF 33

SS 28, RR 51, QQ 10, PP 35, OO 34, NN 48, MM 11

ZZ 44, YY 42, XX 25, WW 20, VV 5, UU 30, TT 6

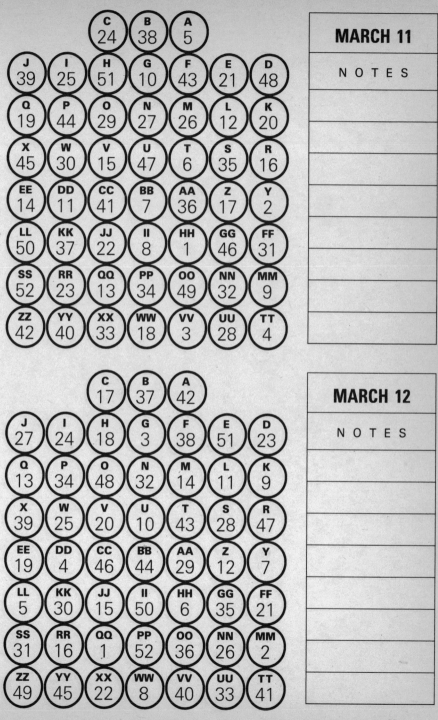

MARCH 11

NOTES

MARCH 12

NOTES

49

MARCH 13

NOTES

C 16 | B 36 | A 41

J 52 | I 23 | H 17 | G 2 | F 49 | E 24 | D 22

Q 8 | P 38 | O 33 | N 31 | M 51 | L 10 | K 13

X 34 | W 48 | V 19 | U 9 | T 42 | S 27 | R 20

EE 18 | DD 3 | CC 45 | BB 43 | AA 28 | Z 47 | Y 6

LL 4 | KK 29 | JJ 14 | II 11 | HH 5 | GG 39 | FF 25

SS 30 | RR 15 | QQ 50 | PP 37 | OO 35 | NN 21 | MM 1

ZZ 46 | YY 44 | XX 26 | WW 12 | VV 7 | UU 32 | TT 40

MARCH 14

NOTES

C 15 | B 35 | A 40

J 37 | I 22 | H 16 | G 1 | F 46 | E 23 | D 26

Q 12 | P 49 | O 32 | N 30 | M 24 | L 9 | K 8

X 38 | W 33 | V 18 | U 13 | T 41 | S 52 | R 19

EE 17 | DD 2 | CC 44 | BB 42 | AA 27 | Z 20 | Y 5

LL 3 | KK 28 | JJ 51 | II 10 | HH 4 | GG 34 | FF 48

SS 29 | RR 14 | QQ 11 | PP 36 | OO 39 | NN 25 | MM 50

ZZ 45 | YY 43 | XX 21 | WW 47 | VV 6 | UU 31 | TT 7

50

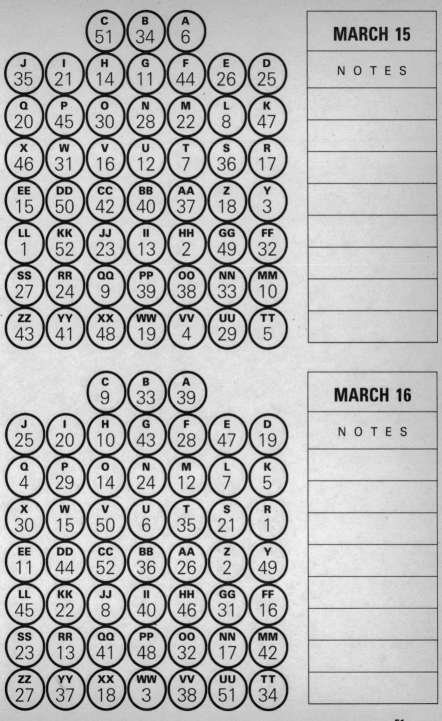

MARCH 15

NOTES

MARCH 16

NOTES

51

MARCH 17

NOTES

C	B	A
13	32	34

J	I	H	G	F	E	D
48	19	9	42	27	20	18

Q	P	O	N	M	L	K
3	28	51	23	47	6	4

X	W	V	U	T	S	R
29	14	11	5	39	25	50

EE	DD	CC	BB	AA	Z	Y
10	43	37	35	21	1	46

LL	KK	JJ	II	HH	GG	FF
44	26	12	7	45	30	15

SS	RR	QQ	PP	OO	NN	MM
22	8	40	33	31	16	41

ZZ	YY	XX	WW	VV	UU	TT
52	36	17	2	49	24	38

MARCH 18

NOTES

C	B	A
8	31	38

J	I	H	G	F	E	D
33	18	13	41	52	19	17

Q	P	O	N	M	L	K
2	27	24	22	20	5	3

X	W	V	U	T	S	R
28	51	10	4	34	48	11

EE	DD	CC	BB	AA	Z	Y
9	42	36	39	25	50	45

LL	KK	JJ	II	HH	GG	FF
43	21	47	6	44	29	14

SS	RR	QQ	PP	OO	NN	MM
26	12	7	32	30	15	40

ZZ	YY	XX	WW	VV	UU	TT
37	35	16	1	46	23	49

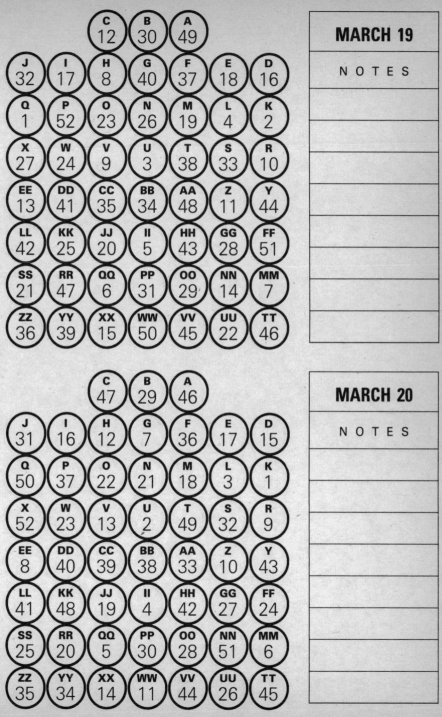

MARCH 19

NOTES

MARCH 20

NOTES

MARCH 21

NOTES

C 20 — B 28 — A 45

J 30	I 15	H 47	G 6	F 35	E 16	D 14
Q 11	P 36	O 26	N 25	M 17	L 2	K 50
X 37	W 22	V 8	U 1	T 46	S 31	R 13
EE 12	DD 7	CC 34	BB 49	AA 32	Z 9	Y 42
LL 40	KK 33	JJ 18	II 3	HH 41	GG 52	FF 23
SS 48	RR 19	QQ 4	PP 29	OO 27	NN 24	MM 5
ZZ 39	YY 38	XX 51	WW 10	VV 43	UU 21	TT 44

MARCH 22

NOTES

C 19 — B 27 — A 44

J 29	I 14	H 20	G 5	F 39	E 15	D 51
Q 10	P 35	O 21	N 48	M 16	L 1	K 11
X 36	W 26	V 12	U 50	T 45	S 30	R 8
EE 47	DD 6	CC 38	BB 46	AA 31	Z 13	Y 41
LL 7	KK 32	JJ 17	II 2	HH 40	GG 37	FF 22
SS 33	RR 18	QQ 3	PP 28	OO 52	NN 23	MM 4
ZZ 34	YY 49	XX 24	WW 9	VV 42	UU 25	TT 43

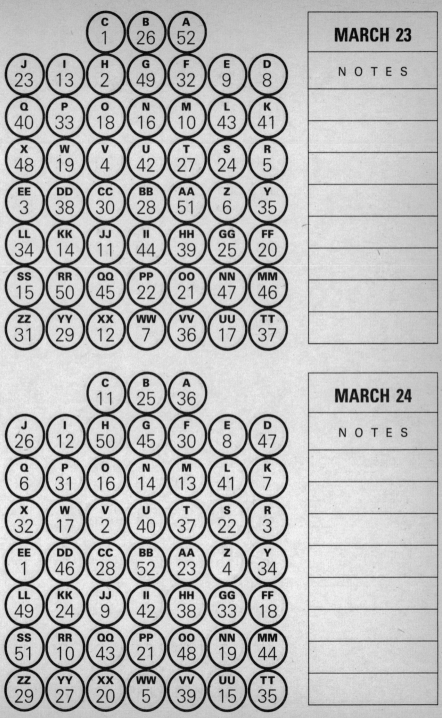

MARCH 23

NOTES

MARCH 24

NOTES

MARCH 25

NOTES

C 4	B 24	A 29

J 14	I 11	H 5	G 39	F 25	E 50	D 10
Q 43	P 21	O 47	N 19	M 1	L 46	K 44
X 26	W 12	V 7	U 45	T 30	S 15	R 40
EE 6	DD 35	CC 33	BB 31	AA 16	Z 41	Y 52
LL 36	KK 17	JJ 2	II 49	HH 37	GG 22	FF 8
SS 18	RR 3	QQ 38	PP 51	OO 23	NN 13	MM 34
ZZ 48	YY 32	XX 9	WW 42	VV 27	UU 20	TT 28

MARCH 26

NOTES

C 3	B 23	A 28

J 51	I 10	H 4	G 34	F 48	E 11	D 9
Q 42	P 25	O 20	N 18	M 50	L 45	K 43
X 21	W 47	V 6	U 44	T 29	S 14	R 7
EE 5	DD 39	CC 32	BB 30	AA 15	Z 40	Y 37
LL 35	KK 16	JJ 1	II 46	HH 36	GG 26	FF 12
SS 17	RR 2	QQ 49	PP 24	OO 22	NN 8	MM 38
ZZ 33	YY 31	XX 13	WW 41	VV 52	UU 19	TT 27

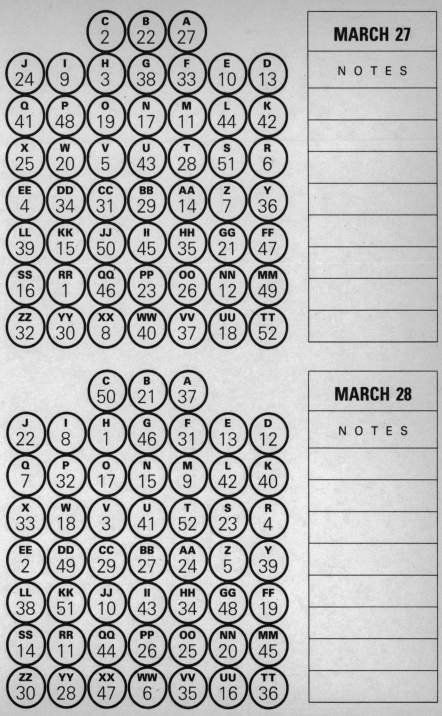

N O T E S

| C 44 | B 20 | A 26 |

| J 12 | I 7 | H 45 | G 30 | F 15 | E 40 | D 6 |

| Q 35 | P 16 | O 1 | N 11 | M 41 | L 52 | K 36 |

| X 17 | W 2 | V 49 | U 37 | T 22 | S 8 | R 38 |

| EE 46 | DD 31 | CC 51 | BB 23 | AA 13 | Z 34 | Y 48 |

| LL 32 | KK 9 | JJ 42 | II 27 | HH 33 | GG 18 | FF 3 |

| SS 10 | RR 43 | QQ 28 | PP 47 | OO 19 | NN 4 | MM 29 |

| ZZ 14 | YY 24 | XX 5 | WW 39 | VV 25 | UU 50 | TT 21 |

N O T E S

| C 43 | B 19 | A 21 |

| J 47 | I 6 | H 44 | G 29 | F 14 | E 7 | D 5 |

| Q 39 | P 15 | O 50 | N 10 | M 40 | L 37 | K 35 |

| X 16 | W 1 | V 46 | U 36 | T 26 | S 12 | R 49 |

| EE 45 | DD 30 | CC 24 | BB 22 | AA 8 | Z 38 | Y 33 |

| LL 31 | KK 13 | JJ 41 | II 52 | HH 32 | GG 17 | FF 2 |

| SS 9 | RR 42 | QQ 27 | PP 20 | OO 18 | NN 3 | MM 28 |

| ZZ 51 | YY 23 | XX 4 | WW 34 | VV 48 | UU 11 | TT 25 |

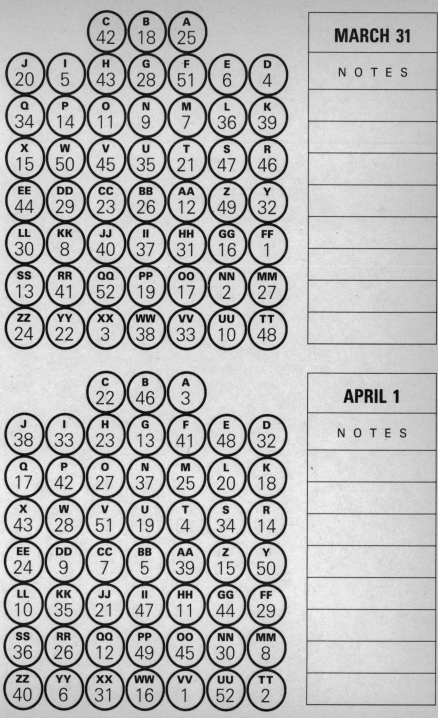

		C 42	B 18	A 25		
J 20	I 5	H 43	G 28	F 51	E 6	D 4
Q 34	P 14	O 11	N 9	M 7	L 36	K 39
X 15	W 50	V 45	U 35	T 21	S 47	R 46
EE 44	DD 29	CC 23	BB 26	AA 12	Z 49	Y 32
LL 30	KK 8	JJ 40	II 37	HH 31	GG 16	FF 1
SS 13	RR 41	QQ 52	PP 19	OO 17	NN 2	MM 27
ZZ 24	YY 22	XX 3	WW 38	VV 33	UU 10	TT 48

MARCH 31

NOTES

		C 22	B 46	A 3		
J 38	I 33	H 23	G 13	F 41	E 48	D 32
Q 17	P 42	O 27	N 37	M 25	L 20	K 18
X 43	W 28	V 51	U 19	T 4	S 34	R 14
EE 24	DD 9	CC 7	BB 5	AA 39	Z 15	Y 50
LL 10	KK 35	JJ 21	II 47	HH 11	GG 44	FF 29
SS 36	RR 26	QQ 12	PP 49	OO 45	NN 30	MM 8
ZZ 40	YY 6	XX 31	WW 16	VV 1	UU 52	TT 2

APRIL 1

NOTES

APRIL 2

NOTES

		C 26	B 45	A 2		
J 49	I 32	H 22	G 8	F 40	E 33	D 31
Q 16	P 41	O 52	N 36	M 48	L 19	K 17
X 42	W 27	V 24	U 18	T 3	S 38	R 51
EE 23	DD 13	CC 6	BB 4	AA 34	Z 14	Y 11
LL 9	KK 39	JJ 25	II 20	HH 10	GG 43	FF 28
SS 35	RR 21	QQ 47	PP 46	OO 44	NN 29	MM 12
ZZ 7	YY 5	XX 30	WW 15	VV 50	UU 37	TT 1

APRIL 3

NOTES

		C 21	B 44	A 1		
J 46	I 31	H 26	G 12	F 7	E 32	D 30
Q 15	P 40	O 37	N 35	M 33	L 18	K 16
X 41	W 52	V 23	U 17	T 2	S 49	R 24
EE 22	DD 8	CC 5	BB 3	AA 38	Z 51	Y 10
LL 13	KK 34	JJ 48	II 19	HH 9	GG 42	FF 27
SS 39	RR 25	QQ 20	PP 45	OO 43	NN 28	MM 47
ZZ 6	YY 4	XX 29	WW 14	VV 11	UU 36	TT 50

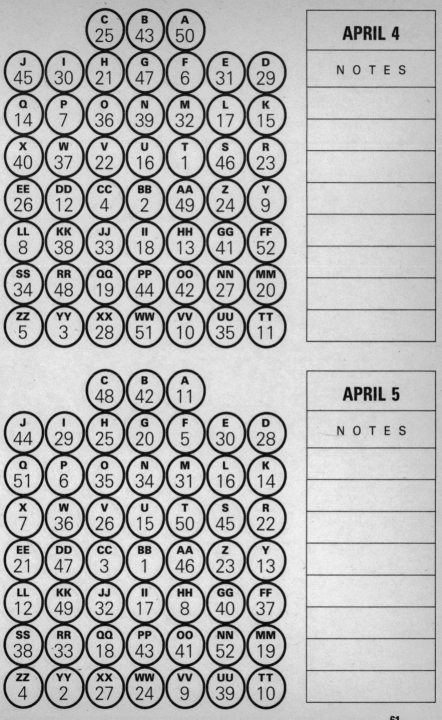

APRIL 4

NOTES

APRIL 5

NOTES

61

APRIL 6

NOTES

| C 33 | B 41 | A 10 |

J 43	I 28	H 48	G 19	F 4	E 29	D 27
Q 24	P 5	O 39	N 38	M 30	L 15	K 51
X 6	W 35	V 21	U 14	T 11	S 44	R 26
EE 25	DD 20	CC 2	BB 50	AA 45	Z 22	Y 8
LL 47	KK 46	JJ 31	II 16	HH 12	GG 7	FF 36
SS 49	RR 32	QQ 17	PP 42	OO 40	NN 37	MM 18
ZZ 3	YY 1	XX 52	WW 23	VV 13	UU 34	TT 9

APRIL 7

NOTES

| C 32 | B 40 | A 9 |

J 42	I 27	H 33	G 18	F 3	E 28	D 52
Q 23	P 4	O 34	N 49	M 29	L 14	K 24
X 5	W 39	V 25	U 51	T 10	S 43	R 21
EE 48	DD 19	CC 1	BB 11	AA 44	Z 26	Y 12
LL 20	KK 45	JJ 30	II 15	HH 47	GG 6	FF 35
SS 46	RR 31	QQ 16	PP 41	OO 7	NN 36	MM 17
ZZ 2	YY 50	XX 37	WW 22	VV 8	UU 38	TT 13

62

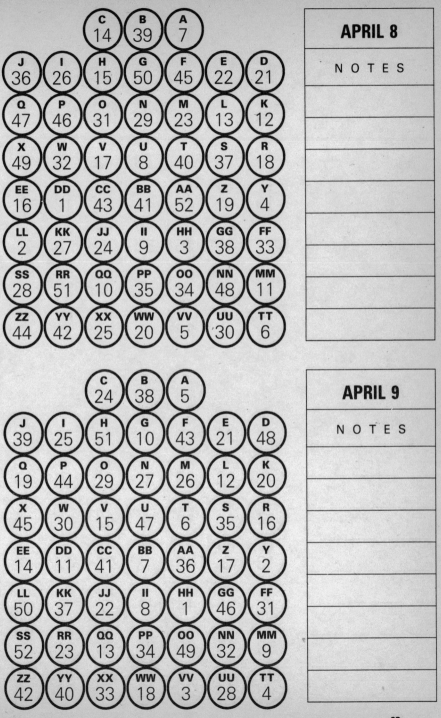

APRIL 8

NOTES

APRIL 9

NOTES

63

APRIL 10

NOTES

(C 17) (B 37) (A 42)

(J 27) (I 24) (H 18) (G 3) (F 38) (E 51) (D 23)

(Q 13) (P 34) (O 48) (N 32) (M 14) (L 11) (K 9)

(X 39) (W 25) (V 20) (U 10) (T 43) (S 28) (R 47)

(EE 19) (DD 4) (CC 46) (BB 44) (AA 29) (Z 12) (Y 7)

(LL 5) (KK 30) (JJ 15) (II 50) (HH 6) (GG 35) (FF 21)

(SS 31) (RR 16) (QQ 1) (PP 52) (OO 36) (NN 26) (MM 2)

(ZZ 49) (YY 45) (XX 22) (WW 8) (VV 40) (UU 33) (TT 41)

APRIL 11

NOTES

(C 16) (B 36) (A 41)

(J 52) (I 23) (H 17) (G 2) (F 49) (E 24) (D 22)

(Q 8) (P 38) (O 33) (N 31) (M 51) (L 10) (K 13)

(X 34) (W 48) (V 19) (U 9) (T 42) (S 27) (R 20)

(EE 18) (DD 3) (CC 45) (BB 43) (AA 28) (Z 47) (Y 6)

(LL 4) (KK 29) (JJ 14) (II 11) (HH 5) (GG 39) (FF 25)

(SS 30) (RR 15) (QQ 50) (PP 37) (OO 35) (NN 21) (MM 1)

(ZZ 46) (YY 44) (XX 26) (WW 12) (VV 7) (UU 32) (TT 40)

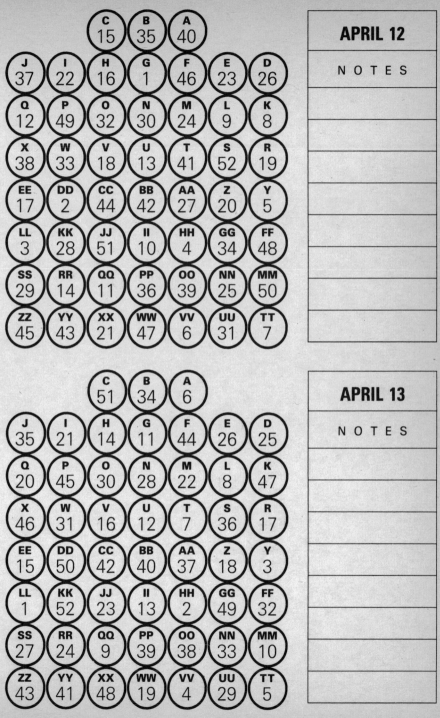

APRIL 14

NOTES

		C 9	B 33	A 39		
J 25	I 20	H 10	G 43	F 28	E 47	D 19
Q 4	P 29	O 14	N 24	M 12	L 7	K 5
X 30	W 15	V 50	U 6	T 35	S 21	R 1
EE 11	DD 44	CC 52	BB 36	AA 26	Z 2	Y 49
LL 45	KK 22	JJ 8	II 40	HH 46	GG 31	FF 16
SS 23	RR 13	QQ 41	PP 48	OO 32	NN 17	MM 42
ZZ 27	YY 37	XX 18	WW 3	VV 38	UU 51	TT 34

APRIL 15

NOTES

		C 13	B 32	A 34		
J 48	I 19	H 9	G 42	F 27	E 20	D 18
Q 3	P 28	O 51	N 23	M 47	L 6	K 4
X 29	W 14	V 11	U 5	T 39	S 25	R 50
EE 10	DD 43	CC 37	BB 35	AA 21	Z 1	Y 46
LL 44	KK 26	JJ 12	II 7	HH 45	GG 30	FF 15
SS 22	RR 8	QQ 40	PP 33	OO 31	NN 16	MM 41
ZZ 52	YY 36	XX 17	WW 2	VV 49	UU 24	TT 38

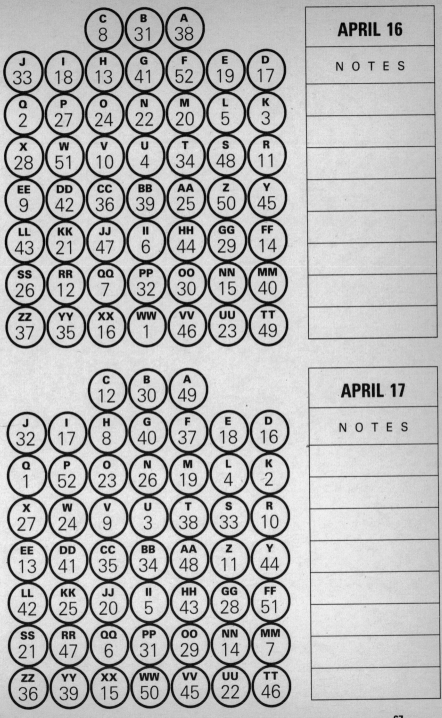

APRIL 16

NOTES

APRIL 17

NOTES

67

APRIL 18

NOTES

		C 47	B 29	A 46		
J 31	I 16	H 12	G 7	F 36	E 17	D 15
Q 50	P 37	O 22	N 21	M 18	L 3	K 1
X 52	W 23	V 13	U 2	T 49	S 32	R 9
EE 8	DD 40	CC 39	BB 38	AA 33	Z 10	Y 43
LL 41	KK 48	JJ 19	II 4	HH 42	GG 27	FF 24
SS 25	RR 20	QQ 5	PP 30	OO 28	NN 51	MM 6
ZZ 35	YY 34	XX 14	WW 11	VV 44	UU 26	TT 45

APRIL 19

NOTES

		C 20	B 28	A 45		
J 30	I 15	H 47	G 6	F 35	E 16	D 14
Q 11	P 36	O 26	N 25	M 17	L 2	K 50
X 37	W 22	V 8	U 1	T 46	S 31	R 13
EE 12	DD 7	CC 34	BB 49	AA 32	Z 9	Y 42
LL 40	KK 33	JJ 18	II 3	HH 41	GG 52	FF 23
SS 48	RR 19	QQ 4	PP 29	OO 27	NN 24	MM 5
ZZ 39	YY 38	XX 51	WW 10	VV 43	UU 21	TT 44

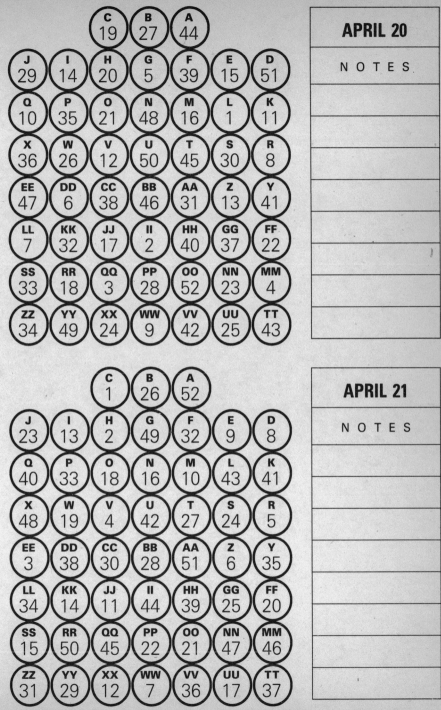

APRIL 22

NOTES

| C 11 | B 25 | A 36 |

J 26	I 12	H 50	G 45	F 30	E 8	D 47
Q 6	P 31	O 16	N 14	M 13	L 41	K 7
X 32	W 17	V 2	U 40	T 37	S 22	R 3
EE 1	DD 46	CC 28	BB 52	AA 23	Z 4	Y 34
LL 49	KK 24	JJ 9	II 42	HH 38	GG 33	FF 18
SS 51	RR 10	QQ 43	PP 21	OO 48	NN 19	MM 44
ZZ 29	YY 27	XX 20	WW 5	VV 39	UU 15	TT 35

APRIL 23

NOTES

| C 4 | B 24 | A 29 |

J 14	I 11	H 5	G 39	F 25	E 50	D 10
Q 43	P 21	O 47	N 19	M 1	L 46	K 44
X 26	W 12	V 7	U 45	T 30	S 15	R 40
EE 6	DD 35	CC 33	BB 31	AA 16	Z 41	Y 52
LL 36	KK 17	JJ 2	II 49	HH 37	GG 22	FF 8
SS 18	RR 3	QQ 38	PP 51	OO 23	NN 13	MM 34
ZZ 48	YY 32	XX 9	WW 42	VV 27	UU 20	TT 28

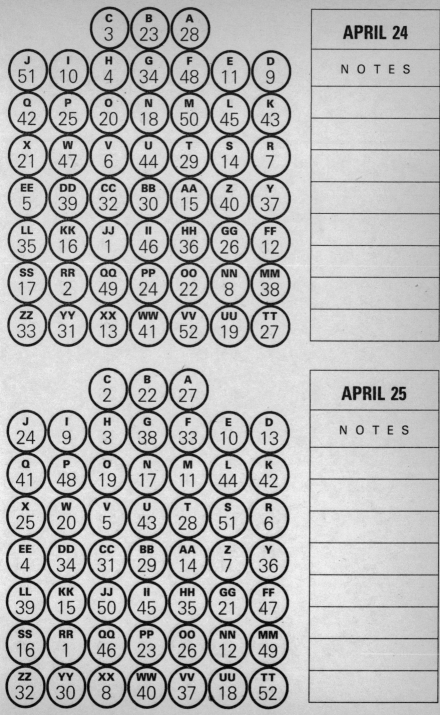

APRIL 24

NOTES

APRIL 25

NOTES

APRIL 26

NOTES

			C 50	B 21	A 37	
J 22	I 8	H 1	G 46	F 31	E 13	D 12
Q 7	P 32	O 17	N 15	M 9	L 42	K 40
X 33	W 18	V 3	U 41	T 52	S 23	R 4
EE 2	DD 49	CC 29	BB 27	AA 24	Z 5	Y 39
LL 38	KK 51	JJ 10	II 43	HH 34	GG 48	FF 19
SS 14	RR 11	QQ 44	PP 26	OO 25	NN 20	MM 45
ZZ 30	YY 28	XX 47	WW 6	VV 35	UU 16	TT 36

APRIL 27

NOTES

			C 44	B 20	A 26	
J 12	I 7	H 45	G 30	F 15	E 40	D 6
Q 35	P 16	O 1	N 11	M 41	L 52	K 36
X 17	W 2	V 49	U 37	T 22	S 8	R 38
EE 46	DD 31	CC 51	BB 23	AA 13	Z 34	Y 48
LL 32	KK 9	JJ 42	II 27	HH 33	GG 18	FF 3
SS 10	RR 43	QQ 28	PP 47	OO 19	NN 4	MM 29
ZZ 14	YY 24	XX 5	WW 39	VV 25	UU 50	TT 21

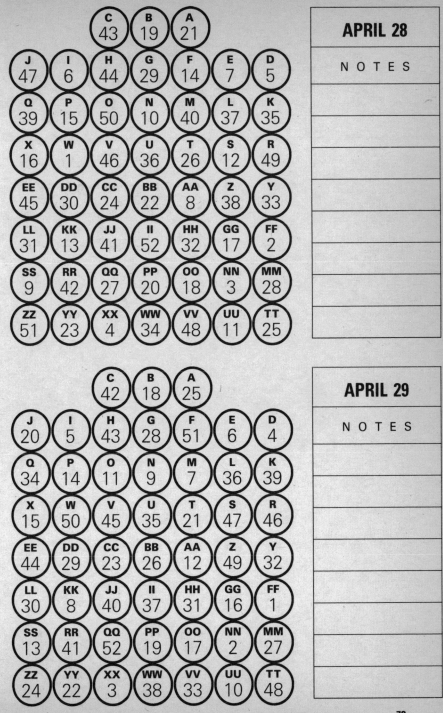

APRIL 30

NOTES

		C 41	B 17	A 48		
J 19	I 4	H 42	G 27	F 24	E 5	D 3
Q 38	P 51	O 10	N 13	M 6	L 35	K 34
X 14	W 11	V 44	U 39	T 25	S 20	R 45
EE 43	DD 28	CC 22	BB 21	AA 47	Z 46	Y 31
LL 29	KK 12	JJ 7	II 36	HH 30	GG 15	FF 50
SS 8	RR 40	QQ 37	PP 18	OO 16	NN 1	MM 52
ZZ 23	YY 26	XX 2	WW 49	VV 32	UU 9	TT 33

MAY 1

NOTES

		C 21	B 44	A 1		
J 46	I 31	H 26	G 12	F 7	E 32	D 30
Q 15	P 40	O 37	N 35	M 33	L 18	K 16
X 41	W 52	V 23	U 17	T 2	S 49	R 24
EE 22	DD 8	CC 5	BB 3	AA 38	Z 51	Y 10
LL 13	KK 34	JJ 48	II 19	HH 9	GG 42	FF 27
SS 39	RR 25	QQ 20	PP 45	OO 43	NN 28	MM 47
ZZ 6	YY 4	XX 29	WW 14	VV 11	UU 36	TT 50

74

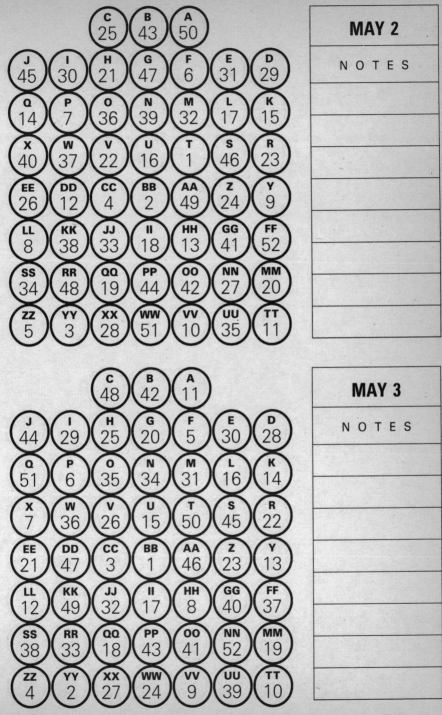

		C 25	B 43	A 50		
J 45	I 30	H 21	G 47	F 6	E 31	D 29
Q 14	P 7	O 36	N 39	M 32	L 17	K 15
X 40	W 37	V 22	U 16	T 1	S 46	R 23
EE 26	DD 12	CC 4	BB 2	AA 49	Z 24	Y 9
LL 8	KK 38	JJ 33	II 18	HH 13	GG 41	FF 52
SS 34	RR 48	QQ 19	PP 44	OO 42	NN 27	MM 20
ZZ 5	YY 3	XX 28	WW 51	VV 10	UU 35	TT 11

MAY 2

NOTES

		C 48	B 42	A 11		
J 44	I 29	H 25	G 20	F 5	E 30	D 28
Q 51	P 6	O 35	N 34	M 31	L 16	K 14
X 7	W 36	V 26	U 15	T 50	S 45	R 22
EE 21	DD 47	CC 3	BB 1	AA 46	Z 23	Y 13
LL 12	KK 49	JJ 32	II 17	HH 8	GG 40	FF 37
SS 38	RR 33	QQ 18	PP 43	OO 41	NN 52	MM 19
ZZ 4	YY 2	XX 27	WW 24	VV 9	UU 39	TT 10

MAY 3

NOTES

MAY 4

NOTES

		C 33	B 41	A 10		
J 43	I 28	H 48	G 19	F 4	E 29	D 27
Q 24	P 5	O 39	N 38	M 30	L 15	K 51
X 6	W 35	V 21	U 14	T 11	S 44	R 26
EE 25	DD 20	CC 2	BB 50	AA 45	Z 22	Y 8
LL 47	KK 46	JJ 31	II 16	HH 12	GG 7	FF 36
SS 49	RR 32	QQ 17	PP 42	OO 40	NN 37	MM 18
ZZ 3	YY 1	XX 52	WW 23	VV 13	UU 34	TT 9

MAY 5

NOTES

		C 32	B 40	A 9		
J 42	I 27	H 33	G 18	F 3	E 28	D 52
Q 23	P 4	O 34	N 49	M 29	L 14	K 24
X 5	W 39	V 25	U 51	T 10	S 43	R 21
EE 48	DD 19	CC 1	BB 11	AA 44	Z 26	Y 12
LL 20	KK 45	JJ 30	II 15	HH 47	GG 6	FF 35
SS 46	RR 31	QQ 16	PP 41	OO 7	NN 36	MM 17
ZZ 2	YY 50	XX 37	WW 22	VV 8	UU 38	TT 13

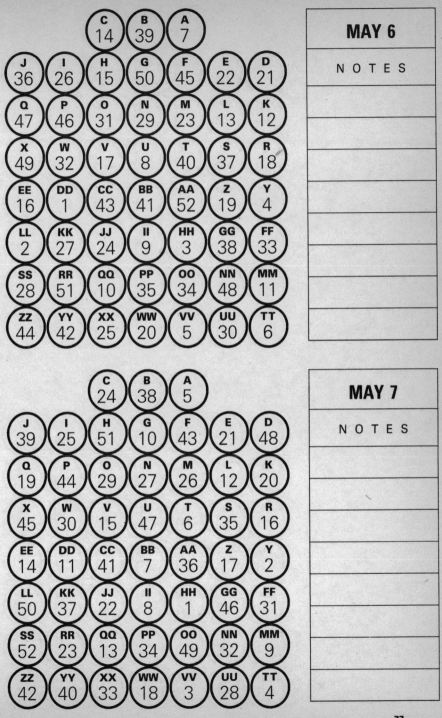

| C | B | A |
| 14 | 39 | 7 |

MAY 6

NOTES

| J | I | H | G | F | E | D |
| 36 | 26 | 15 | 50 | 45 | 22 | 21 |

| Q | P | O | N | M | L | K |
| 47 | 46 | 31 | 29 | 23 | 13 | 12 |

| X | W | V | U | T | S | R |
| 49 | 32 | 17 | 8 | 40 | 37 | 18 |

| EE | DD | CC | BB | AA | Z | Y |
| 16 | 1 | 43 | 41 | 52 | 19 | 4 |

| LL | KK | JJ | II | HH | GG | FF |
| 2 | 27 | 24 | 9 | 3 | 38 | 33 |

| SS | RR | QQ | PP | OO | NN | MM |
| 28 | 51 | 10 | 35 | 34 | 48 | 11 |

| ZZ | YY | XX | WW | VV | UU | TT |
| 44 | 42 | 25 | 20 | 5 | 30 | 6 |

| C | B | A |
| 24 | 38 | 5 |

MAY 7

NOTES

| J | I | H | G | F | E | D |
| 39 | 25 | 51 | 10 | 43 | 21 | 48 |

| Q | P | O | N | M | L | K |
| 19 | 44 | 29 | 27 | 26 | 12 | 20 |

| X | W | V | U | T | S | R |
| 45 | 30 | 15 | 47 | 6 | 35 | 16 |

| EE | DD | CC | BB | AA | Z | Y |
| 14 | 11 | 41 | 7 | 36 | 17 | 2 |

| LL | KK | JJ | II | HH | GG | FF |
| 50 | 37 | 22 | 8 | 1 | 46 | 31 |

| SS | RR | QQ | PP | OO | NN | MM |
| 52 | 23 | 13 | 34 | 49 | 32 | 9 |

| ZZ | YY | XX | WW | VV | UU | TT |
| 42 | 40 | 33 | 18 | 3 | 28 | 4 |

MAY 8

NOTES

		C 17	B 37	A 42		
J 27	I 24	H 18	G 3	F 38	E 51	D 23
Q 13	P 34	O 48	N 32	M 14	L 11	K 9
X 39	W 25	V 20	U 10	T 43	S 28	R 47
EE 19	DD 4	CC 46	BB 44	AA 29	Z 12	Y 7
LL 5	KK 30	JJ 15	II 50	HH 6	GG 35	FF 21
SS 31	RR 16	QQ 1	PP 52	OO 36	NN 26	MM 2
ZZ 49	YY 45	XX 22	WW 8	VV 40	UU 33	TT 41

MAY 9

NOTES

		C 16	B 36	A 41		
J 52	I 23	H 17	G 2	F 49	E 24	D 22
Q 8	P 38	O 33	N 31	M 51	L 10	K 13
X 34	W 48	V 19	U 9	T 42	S 27	R 20
EE 18	DD 3	CC 45	BB 43	AA 28	Z 47	Y 6
LL 4	KK 29	JJ 14	II 11	HH 5	GG 39	FF 25
SS 30	RR 15	QQ 50	PP 37	OO 35	NN 21	MM 1
ZZ 46	YY 44	XX 26	WW 12	VV 7	UU 32	TT 40

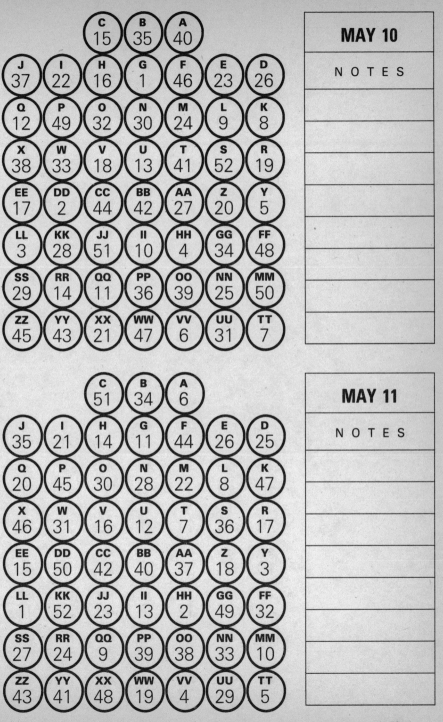

MAY 12

NOTES

		C 9	B 33	A 39		
J 25	I 20	H 10	G 43	F 28	E 47	D 19
Q 4	P 29	O 14	N 24	M 12	L 7	K 5
X 30	W 15	V 50	U 6	T 35	S 21	R 1
EE 11	DD 44	CC 52	BB 36	AA 26	Z 2	Y 49
LL 45	KK 22	JJ 8	II 40	HH 46	GG 31	FF 16
SS 23	RR 13	QQ 41	PP 48	OO 32	NN 17	MM 42
ZZ 27	YY 37	XX 18	WW 3	VV 38	UU 51	TT 34

MAY 13

NOTES

		C 13	B 32	A 34		
J 48	I 19	H 9	G 42	F 27	E 20	D 18
Q 3	P 28	O 51	N 23	M 47	L 6	K 4
X 29	W 14	V 11	U 5	T 39	S 25	R 50
EE 10	DD 43	CC 37	BB 35	AA 21	Z 1	Y 46
LL 44	KK 26	JJ 12	II 7	HH 45	GG 30	FF 15
SS 22	RR 8	QQ 40	PP 33	OO 31	NN 16	MM 41
ZZ 52	YY 36	XX 17	WW 2	VV 49	UU 24	TT 38

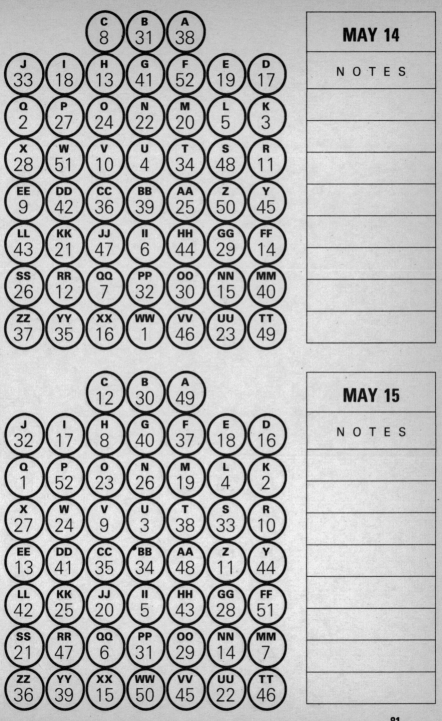

MAY 14

NOTES

MAY 15

NOTES

81

MAY 16

NOTES

		C 47	B 29	A 46		
J 31	I 16	H 12	G 7	F 36	E 17	D 15
Q 50	P 37	O 22	N 21	M 18	L 3	K 1
X 52	W 23	V 13	U 2	T 49	S 32	R 9
EE 8	DD 40	CC 39	BB 38	AA 33	Z 10	Y 43
LL 41	KK 48	JJ 19	II 4	HH 42	GG 27	FF 24
SS 25	RR 20	QQ 5	PP 30	OO 28	NN 51	MM 6
ZZ 35	YY 34	XX 14	WW 11	VV 44	UU 26	TT 45

MAY 17

NOTES

		C 20	B 28	A 45		
J 30	I 15	H 47	G 6	F 35	E 16	D 14
Q 11	P 36	O 26	N 25	M 17	L 2	K 50
X 37	W 22	V 8	U 1	T 46	S 31	R 13
EE 12	DD 7	CC 34	BB 49	AA 32	Z 9	Y 42
LL 40	KK 33	JJ 18	II 3	HH 41	GG 52	FF 23
SS 48	RR 19	QQ 4	PP 29	OO 27	NN 24	MM 5
ZZ 39	YY 38	XX 51	WW 10	VV 43	UU 21	TT 44

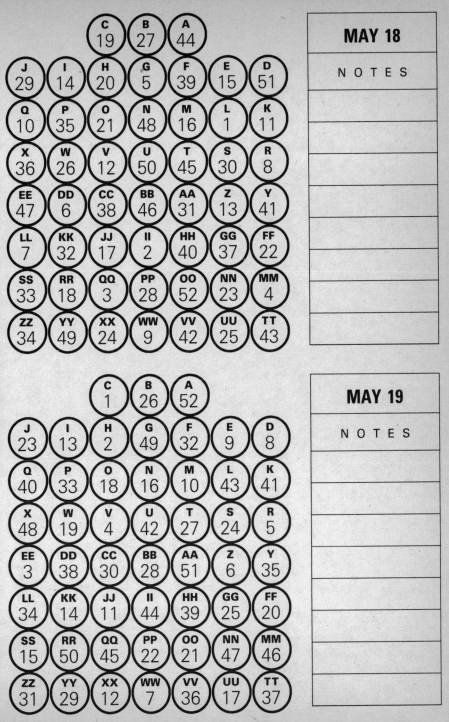

MAY 18

NOTES

MAY 19

NOTES

MAY 20

NOTES

C 11 B 25 A 36

J 26 I 12 H 50 G 45 F 30 E 8 D 47

Q 6 P 31 O 16 N 14 M 13 L 41 K 7

X 32 W 17 V 2 U 40 T 37 S 22 R 3

EE 1 DD 46 CC 28 BB 52 AA 23 Z 4 Y 34

LL 49 KK 24 JJ 9 II 42 HH 38 GG 33 FF 18

SS 51 RR 10 QQ 43 PP 21 OO 48 NN 19 MM 44

ZZ 29 YY 27 XX 20 WW 5 VV 39 UU 15 TT 35

MAY 21

NOTES

C 4 B 24 A 29

J 14 I 11 H 5 G 39 F 25 E 50 D 10

Q 43 P 21 O 47 N 19 M 1 L 46 K 44

X 26 W 12 V 7 U 45 T 30 S 15 R 40

EE 6 DD 35 CC 33 BB 31 AA 16 Z 41 Y 52

LL 36 KK 17 JJ 2 II 49 HH 37 GG 22 FF 8

SS 18 RR 3 QQ 38 PP 51 OO 23 NN 13 MM 34

ZZ 48 YY 32 XX 9 WW 42 VV 27 UU 20 TT 28

84

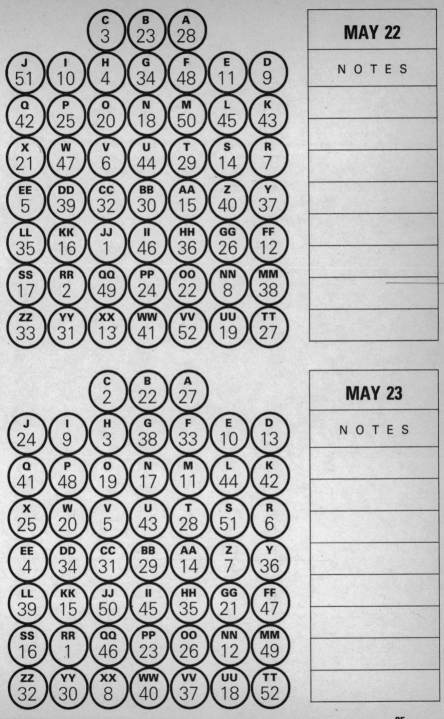

MAY 22

NOTES

MAY 23

NOTES

85

MAY 24

NOTES

		C 50	B 21	A 37		
J 22	I 8	H 1	G 46	F 31	E 13	D 12
Q 7	P 32	O 17	N 15	M 9	L 42	K 40
X 33	W 18	V 3	U 41	T 52	S 23	R 4
EE 2	DD 49	CC 29	BB 27	AA 24	Z 5	Y 39
LL 38	KK 51	JJ 10	II 43	HH 34	GG 48	FF 19
SS 14	RR 11	QQ 44	PP 26	OO 25	NN 20	MM 45
ZZ 30	YY 28	XX 47	WW 6	VV 35	UU 16	TT 36

MAY 25

NOTES

		C 44	B 20	A 26		
J 12	I 7	H 45	G 30	F 15	E 40	D 6
Q 35	P 16	O 1	N 11	M 41	L 52	K 36
X 17	W 2	V 49	U 37	T 22	S 8	R 38
EE 46	DD 31	CC 51	BB 23	AA 13	Z 34	Y 48
LL 32	KK 9	JJ 42	II 27	HH 33	GG 18	FF 3
SS 10	RR 43	QQ 28	PP 47	OO 19	NN 4	MM 29
ZZ 14	YY 24	XX 5	WW 39	VV 25	UU 50	TT 21

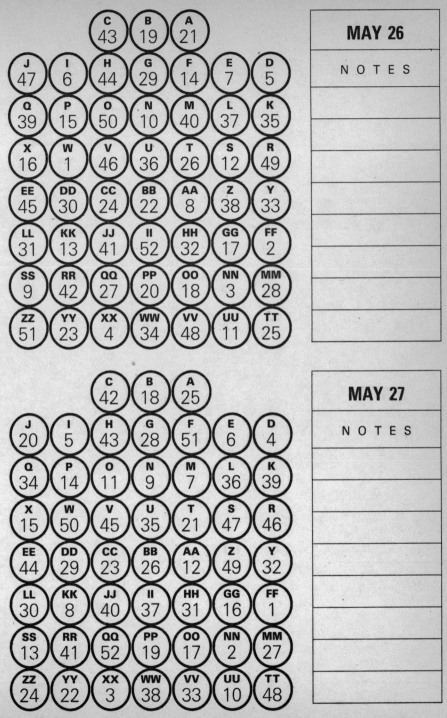

MAY 26

NOTES

MAY 27

NOTES

87

MAY 28

NOTES

C 41 B 17 A 48

J 19 I 4 H 42 G 27 F 24 E 5 D 3

Q 38 P 51 O 10 N 13 M 6 L 35 K 34

X 14 W 11 V 44 U 39 T 25 S 20 R 45

EE 43 DD 28 CC 22 BB 21 AA 47 Z 46 Y 31

LL 29 KK 12 JJ 7 II 36 HH 30 GG 15 FF 50

SS 8 RR 40 QQ 37 PP 18 OO 16 NN 1 MM 52

ZZ 23 YY 26 XX 2 WW 49 VV 32 UU 9 TT 33

MAY 29

NOTES

C 40 B 16 A 33

J 18 I 3 H 41 G 52 F 23 E 4 D 2

Q 49 P 24 O 9 N 8 M 5 L 39 K 38

X 51 W 10 V 43 U 34 T 48 S 19 R 44

EE 42 DD 27 CC 26 BB 25 AA 20 Z 45 Y 30

LL 28 KK 47 JJ 6 II 35 HH 29 GG 14 FF 11

SS 12 RR 7 QQ 36 PP 17 OO 15 NN 50 MM 37

ZZ 22 YY 21 XX 1 WW 46 VV 31 UU 13 TT 32

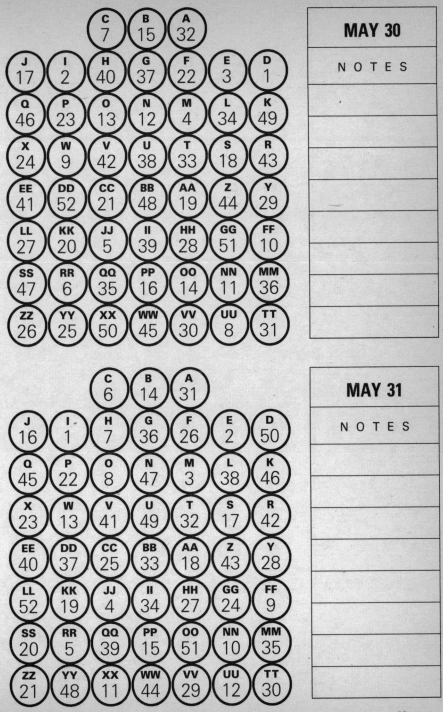

MAY 30

NOTES

MAY 31

NOTES

JUNE 1

NOTES

		C 48	B 42	A 11		
J 44	I 29	H 25	G 20	F 5	E 30	D 28
Q 51	P 6	O 35	N 34	M 31	L 16	K 14
X 7	W 36	V 26	U 15	T 50	S 45	R 22
EE 21	DD 47	CC 3	BB 1	AA 46	Z 23	Y 13
LL 12	KK 49	JJ 32	II 17	HH 8	GG 40	FF 37
SS 38	RR 33	QQ 18	PP 43	OO 41	NN 52	MM 19
ZZ 4	YY 2	XX 27	WW 24	VV 9	UU 39	TT 10

JUNE 2

NOTES

		C 33	B 41	A 10		
J 43	I 28	H 48	G 19	F 4	E 29	D 27
Q 24	P 5	O 39	N 38	M 30	L 15	K 51
X 6	W 35	V 21	U 14	T 11	S 44	R 26
EE 25	DD 20	CC 2	BB 50	AA 45	Z 22	Y 8
LL 47	KK 46	JJ 31	II 16	HH 12	GG 7	FF 36
SS 49	RR 32	QQ 17	PP 42	OO 40	NN 37	MM 18
ZZ 3	YY 1	XX 52	WW 23	VV 13	UU 34	TT 9

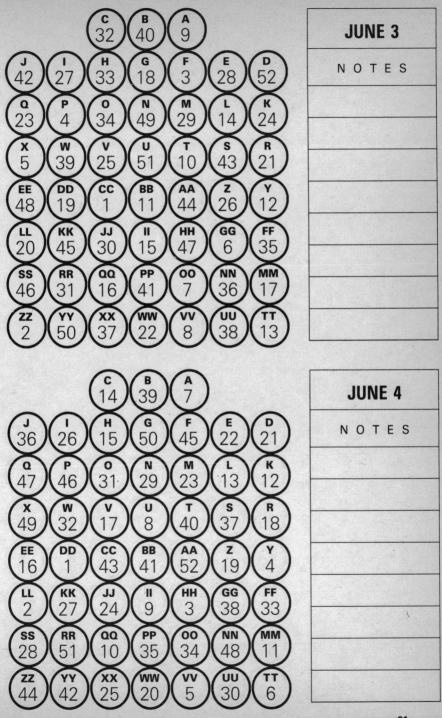

JUNE 3

NOTES

C 32	B 40	A 9	

J 42	I 27	H 33	G 18	F 3	E 28	D 52
Q 23	P 4	O 34	N 49	M 29	L 14	K 24
X 5	W 39	V 25	U 51	T 10	S 43	R 21
EE 48	DD 19	CC 1	BB 11	AA 44	Z 26	Y 12
LL 20	KK 45	JJ 30	II 15	HH 47	GG 6	FF 35
SS 46	RR 31	QQ 16	PP 41	OO 7	NN 36	MM 17
ZZ 2	YY 50	XX 37	WW 22	VV 8	UU 38	TT 13

JUNE 4

NOTES

C 14	B 39	A 7
J 36	I 26	H 15	G 50	F 45	E 22	D 21
Q 47	P 46	O 31	N 29	M 23	L 13	K 12
X 49	W 32	V 17	U 8	T 40	S 37	R 18
EE 16	DD 1	CC 43	BB 41	AA 52	Z 19	Y 4
LL 2	KK 27	JJ 24	II 9	HH 3	GG 38	FF 33
SS 28	RR 51	QQ 10	PP 35	OO 34	NN 48	MM 11
ZZ 44	YY 42	XX 25	WW 20	VV 5	UU 30	TT 6

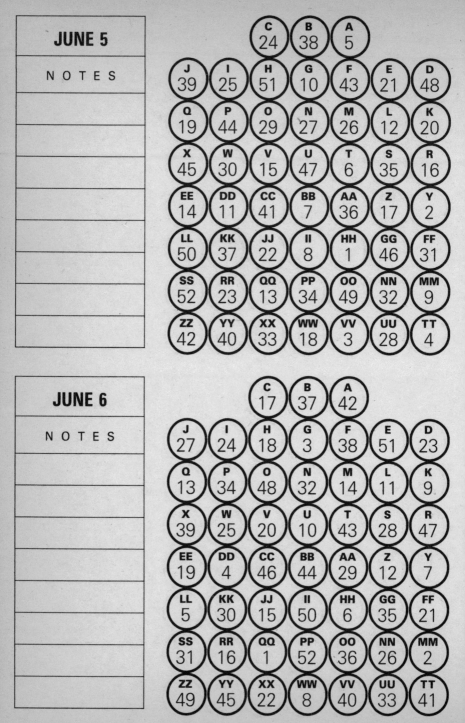

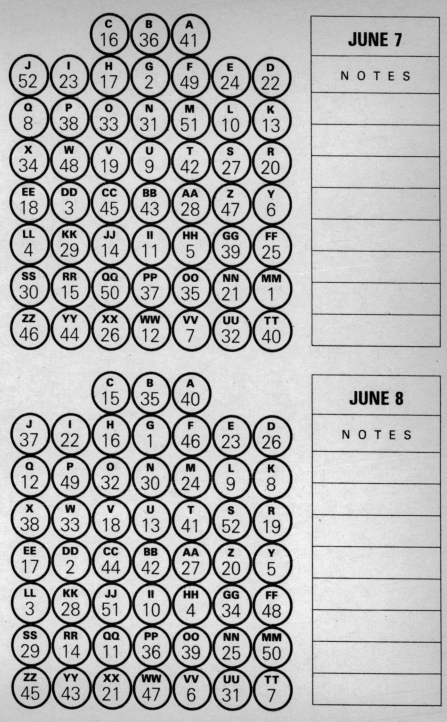

JUNE 7

NOTES

JUNE 8

NOTES

93

JUNE 9

		C 51	B 34	A 6		
J 35	I 21	H 14	G 11	F 44	E 26	D 25
Q 20	P 45	O 30	N 28	M 22	L 8	K 47
X 46	W 31	V 16	U 12	T 7	S 36	R 17
EE 15	DD 50	CC 42	BB 40	AA 37	Z 18	Y 3
LL 1	KK 52	JJ 23	II 13	HH 2	GG 49	FF 32
SS 27	RR 24	QQ 9	PP 39	OO 38	NN 33	MM 10
ZZ 43	YY 41	XX 48	WW 19	VV 4	UU 29	TT 5

JUNE 10

		C 9	B 33	A 39		
J 25	I 20	H 10	G 43	F 28	E 47	D 19
Q 4	P 29	O 14	N 24	M 12	L 7	K 5
X 30	W 15	V 50	U 6	T 35	S 21	R 1
EE 11	DD 44	CC 52	BB 36	AA 26	Z 2	Y 49
LL 45	KK 22	JJ 8	II 40	HH 46	GG 31	FF 16
SS 23	RR 13	QQ 41	PP 48	OO 32	NN 17	MM 42
ZZ 27	YY 37	XX 18	WW 3	VV 38	UU 51	TT 34

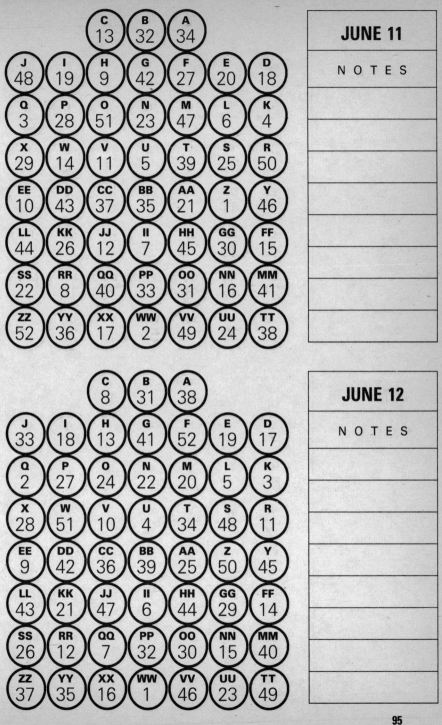

JUNE 11

NOTES

JUNE 12

NOTES

95

JUNE 13

NOTES

		C 12	B 30	A 49		
J 32	I 17	H 8	G 40	F 37	E 18	D 16
Q 1	P 52	O 23	N 26	M 19	L 4	K 2
X 27	W 24	V 9	U 3	T 38	S 33	R 10
EE 13	DD 41	CC 35	BB 34	AA 48	Z 11	Y 44
LL 42	KK 25	JJ 20	II 5	HH 43	GG 28	FF 51
SS 21	RR 47	QQ 6	PP 31	OO 29	NN 14	MM 7
ZZ 36	YY 39	XX 15	WW 50	VV 45	UU 22	TT 46

JUNE 14

NOTES

		C 47	B 29	A 46		
J 31	I 16	H 12	G 7	F 36	E 17	D 15
Q 50	P 37	O 22	N 21	M 18	L 3	K 1
X 52	W 23	V 13	U 2	T 49	S 32	R 9
EE 8	DD 40	CC 39	BB 38	AA 33	Z 10	Y 43
LL 41	KK 48	JJ 19	II 4	HH 42	GG 27	FF 24
SS 25	RR 20	QQ 5	PP 30	OO 28	NN 51	MM 6
ZZ 35	YY 34	XX 14	WW 11	VV 44	UU 26	TT 45

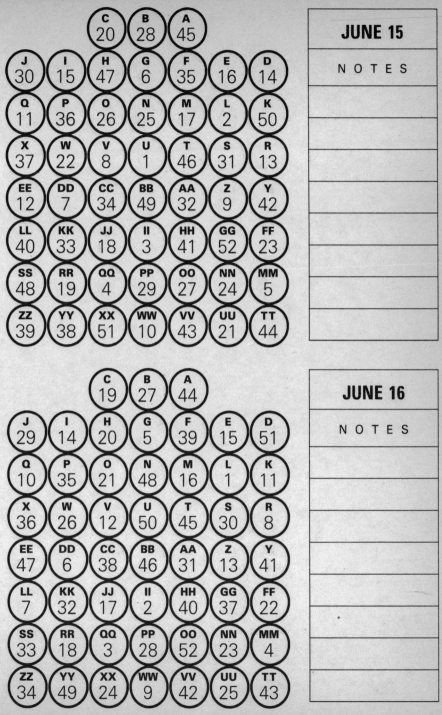

JUNE 15

NOTES

JUNE 16

NOTES

97

JUNE 17

NOTES

		C 1	B 26	A 52		
J 23	I 13	H 2	G 49	F 32	E 9	D 8
Q 40	P 33	O 18	N 16	M 10	L 43	K 41
X 48	W 19	V 4	U 42	T 27	S 24	R 5
EE 3	DD 38	CC 30	BB 28	AA 51	Z 6	Y 35
LL 34	KK 14	JJ 11	II 44	HH 39	GG 25	FF 20
SS 15	RR 50	QQ 45	PP 22	OO 21	NN 47	MM 46
ZZ 31	YY 29	XX 12	WW 7	VV 36	UU 17	TT 37

JUNE 18

NOTES

		C 11	B 25	A 36		
J 26	I 12	H 50	G 45	F 30	E 8	D 47
Q 6	P 31	O 16	N 14	M 13	L 41	K 7
X 32	W 17	V 2	U 40	T 37	S 22	R 3
EE 1	DD 46	CC 28	BB 52	AA 23	Z 4	Y 34
LL 49	KK 24	JJ 9	II 42	HH 38	GG 33	FF 18
SS 51	RR 10	QQ 43	PP 21	OO 48	NN 19	MM 44
ZZ 29	YY 27	XX 20	WW 5	VV 39	UU 15	TT 35

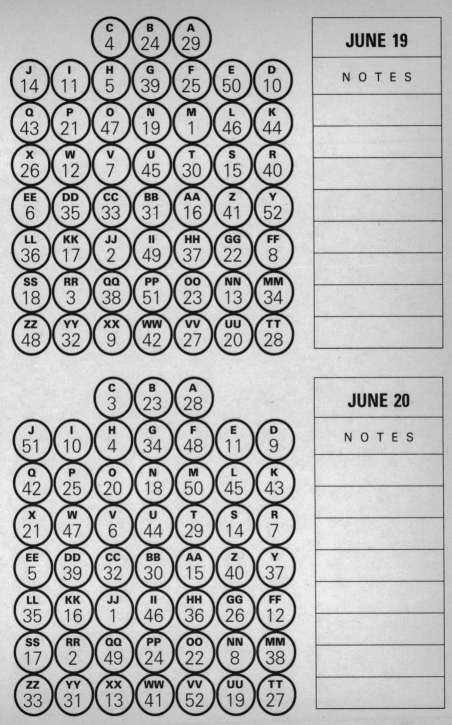

JUNE 21

NOTES

		C 2	B 22	A 27		
J 24	I 9	H 3	G 38	F 33	E 10	D 13
Q 41	P 48	O 19	N 17	M 11	L 44	K 42
X 25	W 20	V 5	U 43	T 28	S 51	R 6
EE 4	DD 34	CC 31	BB 29	AA 14	Z 7	Y 36
LL 39	KK 15	JJ 50	II 45	HH 35	GG 21	FF 47
SS 16	RR 1	QQ 46	PP 23	OO 26	NN 12	MM 49
ZZ 32	YY 30	XX 8	WW 40	VV 37	UU 18	TT 52

JUNE 22

NOTES

		C 50	B 21	A 37		
J 22	I 8	H 1	G 46	F 31	E 13	D 12
Q 7	P 32	O 17	N 15	M 9	L 42	K 40
X 33	W 18	V 3	U 41	T 52	S 23	R 4
EE 2	DD 49	CC 29	BB 27	AA 24	Z 5	Y 39
LL 38	KK 51	JJ 10	II 43	HH 34	GG 48	FF 19
SS 14	RR 11	QQ 44	PP 26	OO 25	NN 20	MM 45
ZZ 30	YY 28	XX 47	WW 6	VV 35	UU 16	TT 36

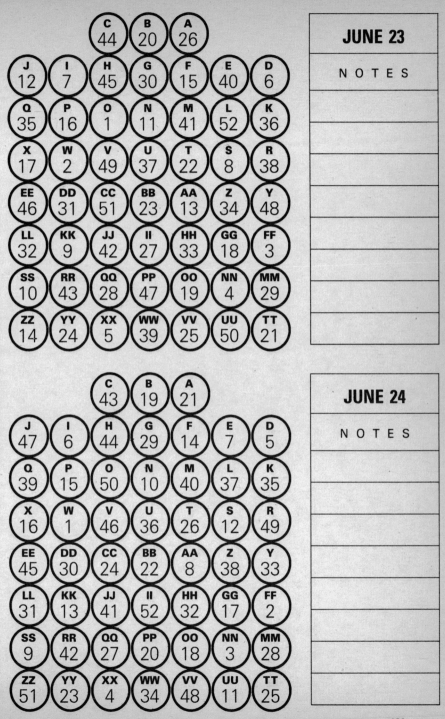

JUNE 25

NOTES

C 42 — B 18 — A 25

J 20 — I 5 — H 43 — G 28 — F 51 — E 6 — D 4

Q 34 — P 14 — O 11 — N 9 — M 7 — L 36 — K 39

X 15 — W 50 — V 45 — U 35 — T 21 — S 47 — R 46

EE 44 — DD 29 — CC 23 — BB 26 — AA 12 — Z 49 — Y 32

LL 30 — KK 8 — JJ 40 — II 37 — HH 31 — GG 16 — FF 1

SS 13 — RR 41 — QQ 52 — PP 19 — OO 17 — NN 2 — MM 27

ZZ 24 — YY 22 — XX 3 — WW 38 — VV 33 — UU 10 — TT 48

JUNE 26

NOTES

C 41 — B 17 — A 48

J 19 — I 4 — H 42 — G 27 — F 24 — E 5 — D 3

Q 38 — P 51 — O 10 — N 13 — M 6 — L 35 — K 34

X 14 — W 11 — V 44 — U 39 — T 25 — S 20 — R 45

EE 43 — DD 28 — CC 22 — BB 21 — AA 47 — Z 46 — Y 31

LL 29 — KK 12 — JJ 7 — II 36 — HH 30 — GG 15 — FF 50

SS 8 — RR 40 — QQ 37 — PP 18 — OO 16 — NN 1 — MM 52

ZZ 23 — YY 26 — XX 2 — WW 49 — VV 32 — UU 9 — TT 33

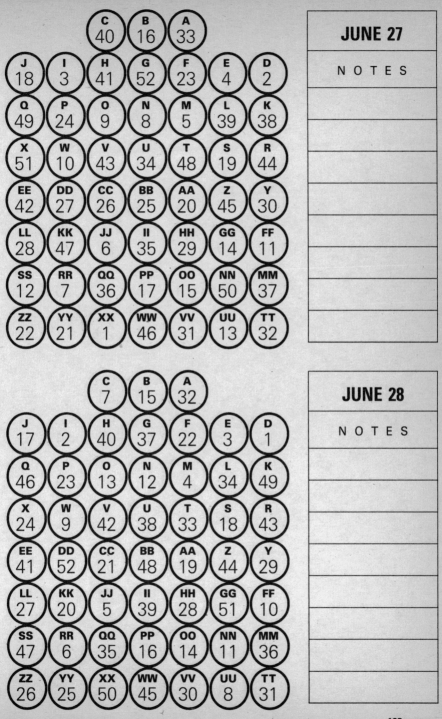

JUNE 27

NOTES

JUNE 28

NOTES

JUNE 29

NOTES

		C 6	B 14	A 31		
J 16	I 1	H 7	G 36	F 26	E 2	D 50
Q 45	P 22	O 8	N 47	M 3	L 38	K 46
X 23	W 13	V 41	U 49	T 32	S 17	R 42
EE 40	DD 37	CC 25	BB 33	AA 18	Z 43	Y 28
LL 52	KK 19	JJ 4	II 34	HH 27	GG 24	FF 9
SS 20	RR 5	QQ 39	PP 15	OO 51	NN 10	MM 35
ZZ 21	YY 48	XX 11	WW 44	VV 29	UU 12	TT 30

JUNE 30

NOTES

		C 38	B 13	A 51		
J 10	I 43	H 34	G 48	F 19	E 44	D 42
Q 27	P 20	O 5	N 3	M 45	L 30	K 28
X 47	W 6	V 35	U 29	T 14	S 11	R 36
EE 39	DD 25	CC 17	BB 15	AA 50	Z 37	Y 22
LL 21	KK 1	JJ 46	II 31	HH 26	GG 12	FF 7
SS 2	RR 49	QQ 32	PP 9	OO 8	NN 40	MM 33
ZZ 18	YY 16	XX 41	WW 52	VV 23	UU 4	TT 24

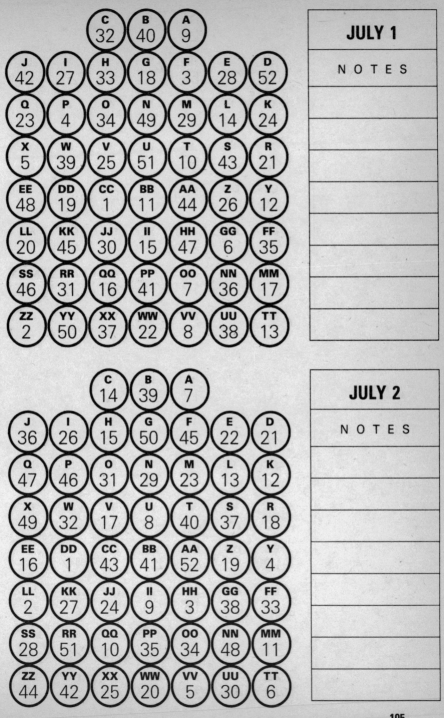

JULY 1

NOTES

JULY 2

NOTES

105

JULY 3

NOTES

			C 24	B 38	A 5	
J 39	I 25	H 51	G 10	F 43	E 21	D 48
Q 19	P 44	O 29	N 27	M 26	L 12	K 20
X 45	W 30	V 15	U 47	T 6	S 35	R 16
EE 14	DD 11	CC 41	BB 7	AA 36	Z 17	Y 2
LL 50	KK 37	JJ 22	II 8	HH 1	GG 46	FF 31
SS 52	RR 23	QQ 13	PP 34	OO 49	NN 32	MM 9
ZZ 42	YY 40	XX 33	WW 18	VV 3	UU 28	TT 4

JULY 4

NOTES

			C 17	B 37	A 42	
J 27	I 24	H 18	G 3	F 38	E 51	D 23
Q 13	P 34	O 48	N 32	M 14	L 11	K 9
X 39	W 25	V 20	U 10	T 43	S 28	R 47
EE 19	DD 4	CC 46	BB 44	AA 29	Z 12	Y 7
LL 5	KK 30	JJ 15	II 50	HH 6	GG 35	FF 21
SS 31	RR 16	QQ 1	PP 52	OO 36	NN 26	MM 2
ZZ 49	YY 45	XX 22	WW 8	VV 40	UU 33	TT 41

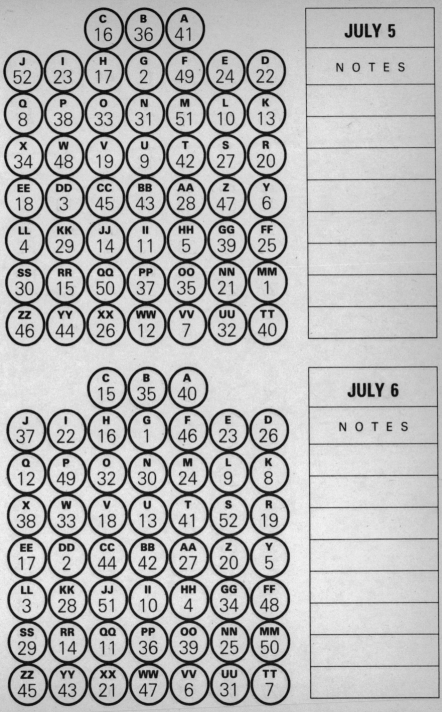

JULY 5

NOTES

JULY 6

NOTES

107

JULY 7

NOTES

C 51	B 34	A 6

J 35	I 21	H 14	G 11	F 44	E 26	D 25
Q 20	P 45	O 30	N 28	M 22	L 8	K 47
X 46	W 31	V 16	U 12	T 7	S 36	R 17
EE 15	DD 50	CC 42	BB 40	AA 37	Z 18	Y 3
LL 1	KK 52	JJ 23	II 13	HH 2	GG 49	FF 32
SS 27	RR 24	QQ 9	PP 39	OO 38	NN 33	MM 10
ZZ 43	YY 41	XX 48	WW 19	VV 4	UU 29	TT 5

JULY 8

NOTES

C 9	B 33	A 39

J 25	I 20	H 10	G 43	F 28	E 47	D 19
Q 4	P 29	O 14	N 24	M 12	L 7	K 5
X 30	W 15	V 50	U 6	T 35	S 21	R 1
EE 11	DD 44	CC 52	BB 36	AA 26	Z 2	Y 49
LL 45	KK 22	JJ 8	II 40	HH 46	GG 31	FF 16
SS 23	RR 13	QQ 41	PP 48	OO 32	NN 17	MM 42
ZZ 27	YY 37	XX 18	WW 3	VV 38	UU 51	TT 34

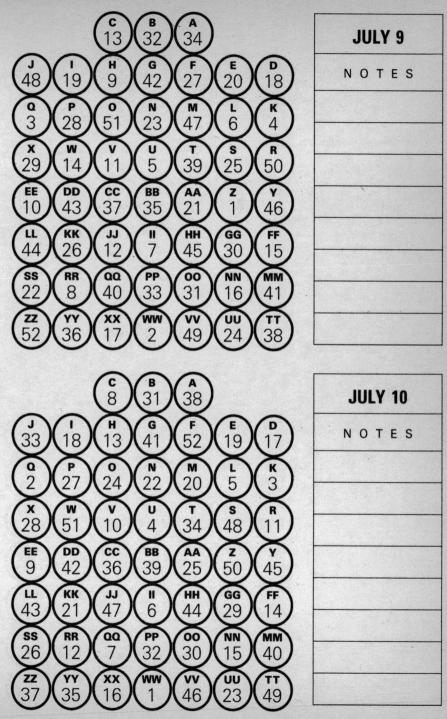

JULY 11

NOTES

		C 12	B 30	A 49		
J 32	I 17	H 8	G 40	F 37	E 18	D 16
Q 1	P 52	O 23	N 26	M 19	L 4	K 2
X 27	W 24	V 9	U 3	T 38	S 33	R 10
EE 13	DD 41	CC 35	BB 34	AA 48	Z 11	Y 44
LL 42	KK 25	JJ 20	II 5	HH 43	GG 28	FF 51
SS 21	RR 47	QQ 6	PP 31	OO 29	NN 14	MM 7
ZZ 36	YY 39	XX 15	WW 50	VV 45	UU 22	TT 46

JULY 12

NOTES

		C 47	B 29	A 46		
J 31	I 16	H 12	G 7	F 36	E 17	D 15
Q 50	P 37	O 22	N 21	M 18	L 3	K 1
X 52	W 23	V 13	U 2	T 49	S 32	R 9
EE 8	DD 40	CC 39	BB 38	AA 33	Z 10	Y 43
LL 41	KK 48	JJ 19	II 4	HH 42	GG 27	FF 24
SS 25	RR 20	QQ 5	PP 30	OO 28	NN 51	MM 6
ZZ 35	YY 34	XX 14	WW 11	VV 44	UU 26	TT 45

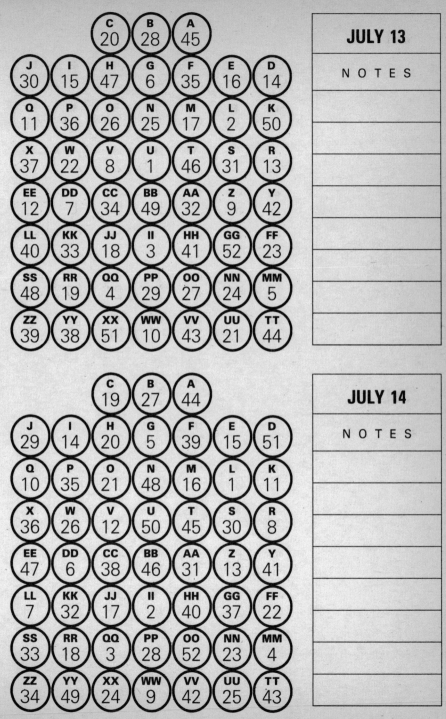

JULY 13

NOTES

JULY 14

NOTES

JULY 15

NOTES

		C 1	B 26	A 52		
J 23	I 13	H 2	G 49	F 32	E 9	D 8
Q 40	P 33	O 18	N 16	M 10	L 43	K 41
X 48	W 19	V 4	U 42	T 27	S 24	R 5
EE 3	DD 38	CC 30	BB 28	AA 51	Z 6	Y 35
LL 34	KK 14	JJ 11	II 44	HH 39	GG 25	FF 20
SS 15	RR 50	QQ 45	PP 22	OO 21	NN 47	MM 46
ZZ 31	YY 29	XX 12	WW 7	VV 36	UU 17	TT 37

JULY 16

NOTES

		C 11	B 25	A 36		
J 26	I 12	H 50	G 45	F 30	E 8	D 47
Q 6	P 31	O 16	N 14	M 13	L 41	K 7
X 32	W 17	V 2	U 40	T 37	S 22	R 3
EE 1	DD 46	CC 28	BB 52	AA 23	Z 4	Y 34
LL 49	KK 24	JJ 9	II 42	HH 38	GG 33	FF 18
SS 51	RR 10	QQ 43	PP 21	OO 48	NN 19	MM 44
ZZ 29	YY 27	XX 20	WW 5	VV 39	UU 15	TT 35

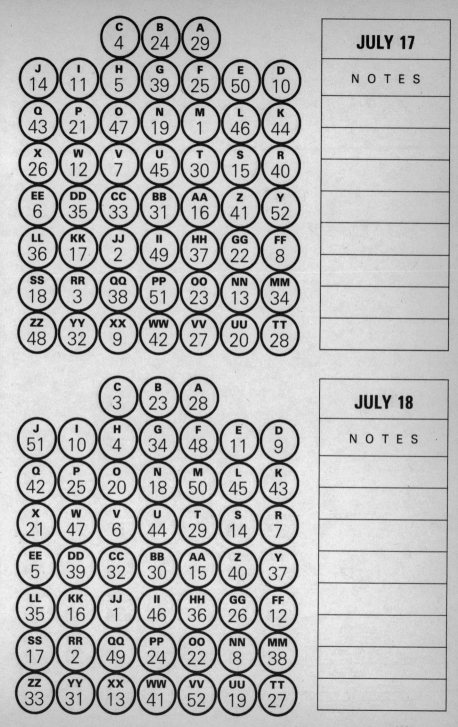

JULY 17

NOTES

JULY 18

NOTES

113

JULY 19

NOTES

		C 2	B 22	A 27		
J 24	I 9	H 3	G 38	F 33	E 10	D 13
Q 41	P 48	O 19	N 17	M 11	L 44	K 42
X 25	W 20	V 5	U 43	T 28	S 51	R 6
EE 4	DD 34	CC 31	BB 29	AA 14	Z 7	Y 36
LL 39	KK 15	JJ 50	II 45	HH 35	GG 21	FF 47
SS 16	RR 1	QQ 46	PP 23	OO 26	NN 12	MM 49
ZZ 32	YY 30	XX 8	WW 40	VV 37	UU 18	TT 52

JULY 20

NOTES

		C 50	B 21	A 37		
J 22	I 8	H 1	G 46	F 31	E 13	D 12
Q 7	P 32	O 17	N 15	M 9	L 42	K 40
X 33	W 18	V 3	U 41	T 52	S 23	R 4
EE 2	DD 49	CC 29	BB 27	AA 24	Z 5	Y 39
LL 38	KK 51	JJ 10	II 43	HH 34	GG 48	FF 19
SS 14	RR 11	QQ 44	PP 26	OO 25	NN 20	MM 45
ZZ 30	YY 28	XX 47	WW 6	VV 35	UU 16	TT 36

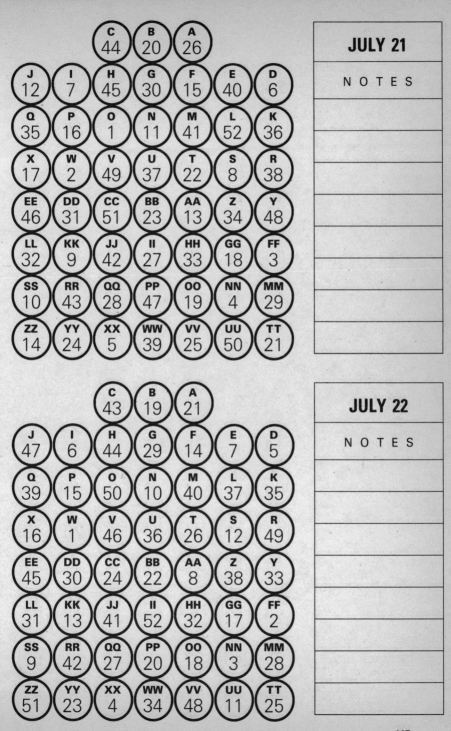

		C 44	B 20	A 26		
J 12	I 7	H 45	G 30	F 15	E 40	D 6
Q 35	P 16	O 1	N 11	M 41	L 52	K 36
X 17	W 2	V 49	U 37	T 22	S 8	R 38
EE 46	DD 31	CC 51	BB 23	AA 13	Z 34	Y 48
LL 32	KK 9	JJ 42	II 27	HH 33	GG 18	FF 3
SS 10	RR 43	QQ 28	PP 47	OO 19	NN 4	MM 29
ZZ 14	YY 24	XX 5	WW 39	VV 25	UU 50	TT 21

JULY 21

NOTES

		C 43	B 19	A 21		
J 47	I 6	H 44	G 29	F 14	E 7	D 5
Q 39	P 15	O 50	N 10	M 40	L 37	K 35
X 16	W 1	V 46	U 36	T 26	S 12	R 49
EE 45	DD 30	CC 24	BB 22	AA 8	Z 38	Y 33
LL 31	KK 13	JJ 41	II 52	HH 32	GG 17	FF 2
SS 9	RR 42	QQ 27	PP 20	OO 18	NN 3	MM 28
ZZ 51	YY 23	XX 4	WW 34	VV 48	UU 11	TT 25

JULY 22

NOTES

JULY 23

NOTES

C 42 B 18 A 25

J 20 I 5 H 43 G 28 F 51 E 6 D 4

Q 34 P 14 O 11 N 9 M 7 L 36 K 39

X 15 W 50 V 45 U 35 T 21 S 47 R 46

EE 44 DD 29 CC 23 BB 26 AA 12 Z 49 Y 32

LL 30 KK 8 JJ 40 II 37 HH 31 GG 16 FF 1

SS 13 RR 41 QQ 52 PP 19 OO 17 NN 2 MM 27

ZZ 24 YY 22 XX 3 WW 38 VV 33 UU 10 TT 48

JULY 24

NOTES

C 41 B 17 A 48

J 19 I 4 H 42 G 27 F 24 E 5 D 3

Q 38 P 51 O 10 N 13 M 6 L 35 K 34

X 14 W 11 V 44 U 39 T 25 S 20 R 45

EE 43 DD 28 CC 22 BB 21 AA 47 Z 46 Y 31

LL 29 KK 12 JJ 7 II 36 HH 30 GG 15 FF 50

SS 8 RR 40 QQ 37 PP 18 OO 16 NN 1 MM 52

ZZ 23 YY 26 XX 2 WW 49 VV 32 UU 9 TT 33

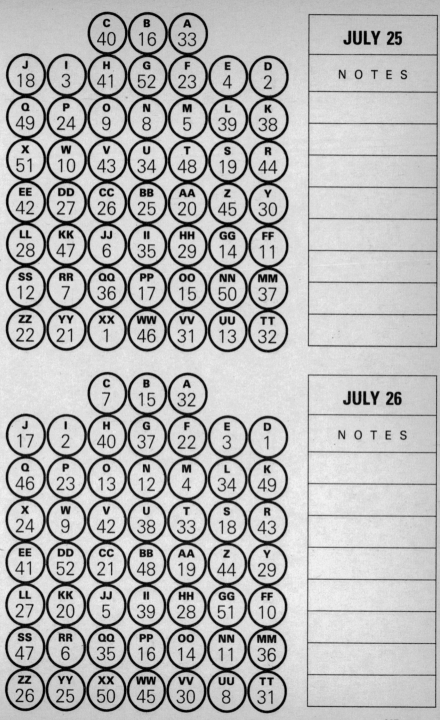

JULY 25

NOTES

JULY 26

NOTES

JULY 27

NOTES

		C 6	B 14	A 31		
J 16	I 1	H 7	G 36	F 26	E 2	D 50
Q 45	P 22	O 8	N 47	M 3	L 38	K 46
X 23	W 13	V 41	U 49	T 32	S 17	R 42
EE 40	DD 37	CC 25	BB 33	AA 18	Z 43	Y 28
LL 52	KK 19	JJ 4	II 34	HH 27	GG 24	FF 9
SS 20	RR 5	QQ 39	PP 15	OO 51	NN 10	MM 35
ZZ 21	YY 48	XX 11	WW 44	VV 29	UU 12	TT 30

JULY 28

NOTES

		C 38	B 13	A 51		
J 10	I 43	H 34	G 48	F 19	E 44	D 42
Q 27	P 20	O 5	N 3	M 45	L 30	K 28
X 47	W 6	V 35	U 29	T 14	S 11	R 36
EE 39	DD 25	CC 17	BB 15	AA 50	Z 37	Y 22
LL 21	KK 1	JJ 46	II 31	HH 26	GG 12	FF 7
SS 2	RR 49	QQ 32	PP 9	OO 8	NN 40	MM 33
ZZ 18	YY 16	XX 41	WW 52	VV 23	UU 4	TT 24

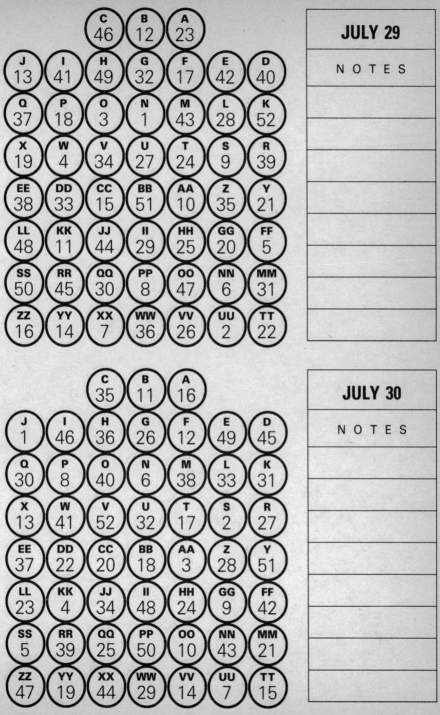

JULY 29

N O T E S

JULY 30

N O T E S

119

JULY 31

NOTES

		C 39	B 10	A 15		
J 50	I 45	H 35	G 21	F 47	E 46	D 44
Q 29	P 12	O 7	N 5	M 49	L 32	K 30
X 8	W 40	V 37	U 31	T 16	S 1	R 52
EE 36	DD 26	CC 19	BB 17	AA 2	Z 27	Y 24
LL 22	KK 3	JJ 38	II 33	HH 23	GG 13	FF 41
SS 4	RR 34	QQ 48	PP 11	OO 9	NN 42	MM 25
ZZ 20	YY 18	XX 43	WW 28	VV 51	UU 6	TT 14

AUGUST 1

NOTES

		C 24	B 38	A 5		
J 39	I 25	H 51	G 10	F 43	E 21	D 48
Q 19	P 44	O 29	N 27	M 26	L 12	K 20
X 45	W 30	V 15	U 47	T 6	S 35	R 16
EE 14	DD 11	CC 41	BB 7	AA 36	Z 17	Y 2
LL 50	KK 37	JJ 22	II 8	HH 1	GG 46	FF 31
SS 52	RR 23	QQ 13	PP 34	OO 49	NN 32	MM 9
ZZ 42	YY 40	XX 33	WW 18	VV 3	UU 28	TT 4

120

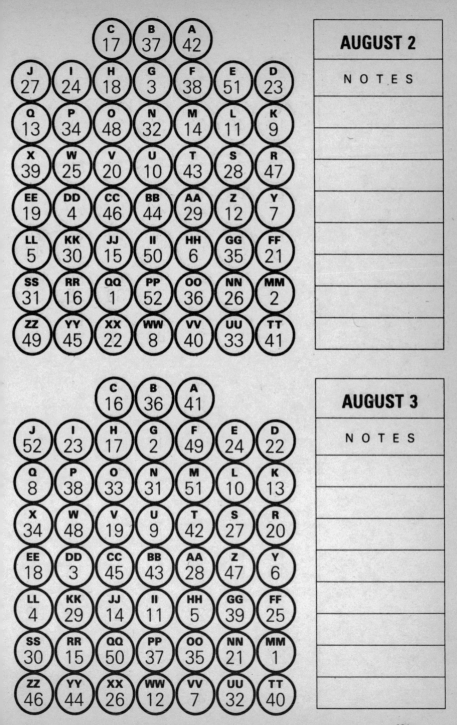

AUGUST 2

NOTES

AUGUST 3

NOTES

121

AUGUST 4

NOTES

C 15 · B 35 · A 40

J 37 · I 22 · H 16 · G 1 · F 46 · E 23 · D 26

Q 12 · P 49 · O 32 · N 30 · M 24 · L 9 · K 8

X 38 · W 33 · V 18 · U 13 · T 41 · S 52 · R 19

EE 17 · DD 2 · CC 44 · BB 42 · AA 27 · Z 20 · Y 5

LL 3 · KK 28 · JJ 51 · II 10 · HH 4 · GG 34 · FF 48

SS 29 · RR 14 · QQ 11 · PP 36 · OO 39 · NN 25 · MM 50

ZZ 45 · YY 43 · XX 21 · WW 47 · VV 6 · UU 31 · TT 7

AUGUST 5

NOTES

C 51 · B 34 · A 6

J 35 · I 21 · H 14 · G 11 · F 44 · E 26 · D 25

Q 20 · P 45 · O 30 · N 28 · M 22 · L 8 · K 47

X 46 · W 31 · V 16 · U 12 · T 7 · S 36 · R 17

EE 15 · DD 50 · CC 42 · BB 40 · AA 37 · Z 18 · Y 3

LL 1 · KK 52 · JJ 23 · II 13 · HH 2 · GG 49 · FF 32

SS 27 · RR 24 · QQ 9 · PP 39 · OO 38 · NN 33 · MM 10

ZZ 43 · YY 41 · XX 48 · WW 19 · VV 4 · UU 29 · TT 5

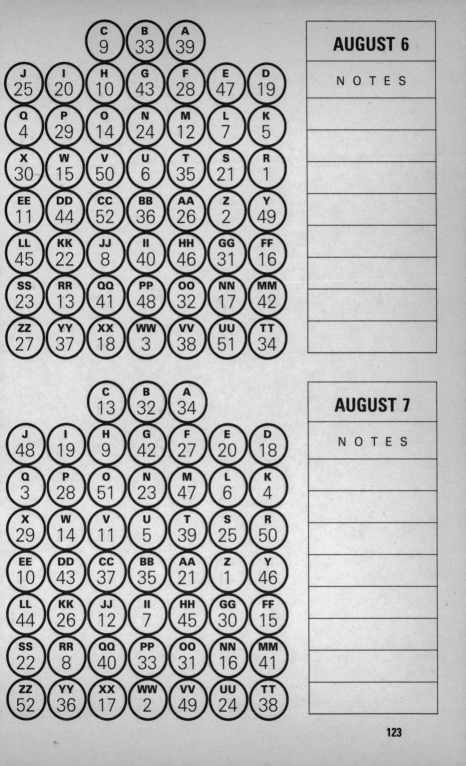

AUGUST 8

NOTES

		C 8	B 31	A 38		
J 33	I 18	H 13	G 41	F 52	E 19	D 17
Q 2	P 27	O 24	N 22	M 20	L 5	K 3
X 28	W 51	V 10	U 4	T 34	S 48	R 11
EE 9	DD 42	CC 36	BB 39	AA 25	Z 50	Y 45
LL 43	KK 21	JJ 47	II 6	HH 44	GG 29	FF 14
SS 26	RR 12	QQ 7	PP 32	OO 30	NN 15	MM 40
ZZ 37	YY 35	XX 16	WW 1	VV 46	UU 23	TT 49

AUGUST 9

NOTES

		C 12	B 30	A 49		
J 32	I 17	H 8	G 40	F 37	E 18	D 16
Q 1	P 52	O 23	N 26	M 19	L 4	K 2
X 27	W 24	V 9	U 3	T 38	S 33	R 10
EE 13	DD 41	CC 35	BB 34	AA 48	Z 11	Y 44
LL 42	KK 25	JJ 20	II 5	HH 43	GG 28	FF 51
SS 21	RR 47	QQ 6	PP 31	OO 29	NN 14	MM 7
ZZ 36	YY 39	XX 15	WW 50	VV 45	UU 22	TT 46

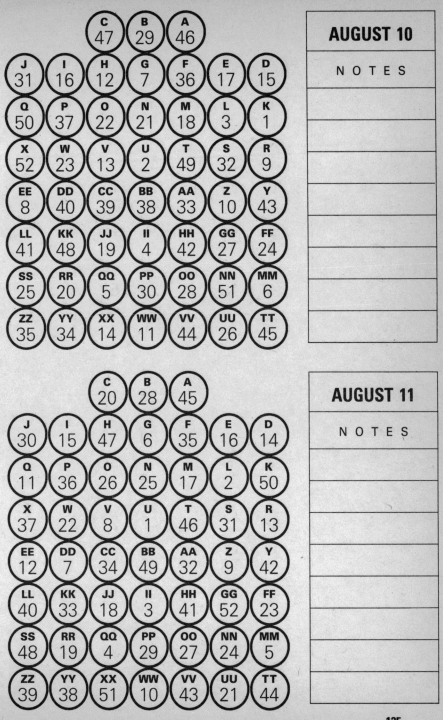

AUGUST 10

NOTES

AUGUST 11

NOTES

AUGUST 12

NOTES

C 19 · B 27 · A 44

J 29	I 14	H 20	G 5	F 39	E 15	D 51
Q 10	P 35	O 21	N 48	M 16	L 1	K 11
X 36	W 26	V 12	U 50	T 45	S 30	R 8
EE 47	DD 6	CC 38	BB 46	AA 31	Z 13	Y 41
LL 7	KK 32	JJ 17	II 2	HH 40	GG 37	FF 22
SS 33	RR 18	QQ 3	PP 28	OO 52	NN 23	MM 4
ZZ 34	YY 49	XX 24	WW 9	VV 42	UU 25	TT 43

AUGUST 13

NOTES

C 1 · B 26 · A 52

J 23	I 13	H 2	G 49	F 32	E 9	D 8
Q 40	P 33	O 18	N 16	M 10	L 43	K 41
X 48	W 19	V 4	U 42	T 27	S 24	R 5
EE 3	DD 38	CC 30	BB 28	AA 51	Z 6	Y 35
LL 34	KK 14	JJ 11	II 44	HH 39	GG 25	FF 20
SS 15	RR 50	QQ 45	PP 22	OO 21	NN 47	MM 46
ZZ 31	YY 29	XX 12	WW 7	VV 36	UU 17	TT 37

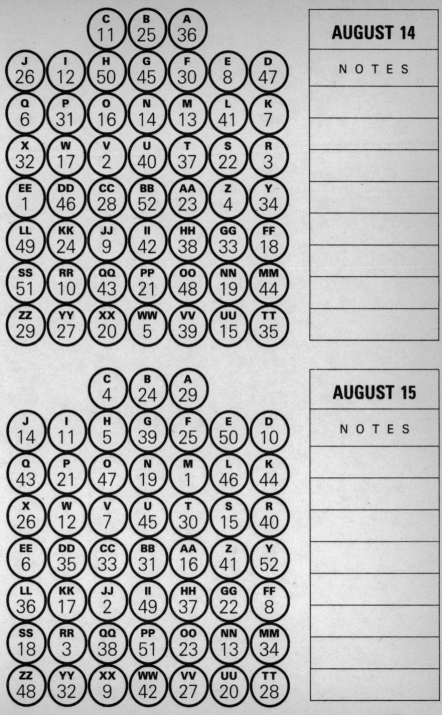

AUGUST 14

NOTES

AUGUST 15

NOTES

127

AUGUST 16

NOTES

		C 3	B 23	A 28		
J 51	I 10	H 4	G 34	F 48	E 11	D 9
Q 42	P 25	O 20	N 18	M 50	L 45	K 43
X 21	W 47	V 6	U 44	T 29	S 14	R 7
EE 5	DD 39	CC 32	BB 30	AA 15	Z 40	Y 37
LL 35	KK 16	JJ 1	II 46	HH 36	GG 26	FF 12
SS 17	RR 2	QQ 49	PP 24	OO 22	NN 8	MM 38
ZZ 33	YY 31	XX 13	WW 41	VV 52	UU 19	TT 27

AUGUST 17

NOTES

		C 2	B 22	A 27		
J 24	I 9	H 3	G 38	F 33	E 10	D 13
Q 41	P 48	O 19	N 17	M 11	L 44	K 42
X 25	W 20	V 5	U 43	T 28	S 51	R 6
EE 4	DD 34	CC 31	BB 29	AA 14	Z 7	Y 36
LL 39	KK 15	JJ 50	II 45	HH 35	GG 21	FF 47
SS 16	RR 1	QQ 46	PP 23	OO 26	NN 12	MM 49
ZZ 32	YY 30	XX 8	WW 40	VV 37	UU 18	TT 52

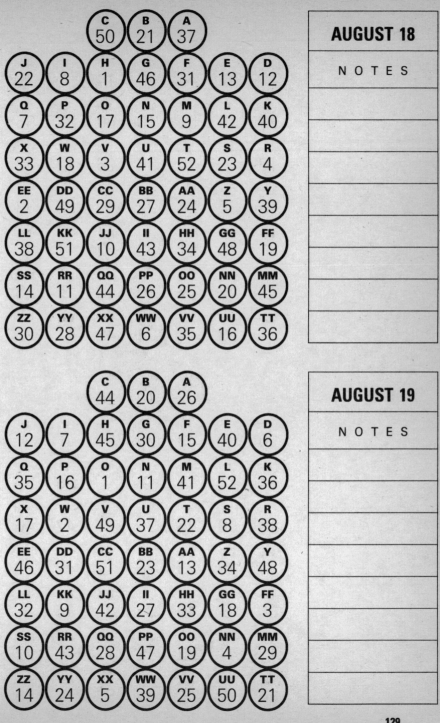

		C 50	B 21	A 37		
J 22	I 8	H 1	G 46	F 31	E 13	D 12
Q 7	P 32	O 17	N 15	M 9	L 42	K 40
X 33	W 18	V 3	U 41	T 52	S 23	R 4
EE 2	DD 49	CC 29	BB 27	AA 24	Z 5	Y 39
LL 38	KK 51	JJ 10	II 43	HH 34	GG 48	FF 19
SS 14	RR 11	QQ 44	PP 26	OO 25	NN 20	MM 45
ZZ 30	YY 28	XX 47	WW 6	VV 35	UU 16	TT 36

AUGUST 18

NOTES

		C 44	B 20	A 26		
J 12	I 7	H 45	G 30	F 15	E 40	D 6
Q 35	P 16	O 1	N 11	M 41	L 52	K 36
X 17	W 2	V 49	U 37	T 22	S 8	R 38
EE 46	DD 31	CC 51	BB 23	AA 13	Z 34	Y 48
LL 32	KK 9	JJ 42	II 27	HH 33	GG 18	FF 3
SS 10	RR 43	QQ 28	PP 47	OO 19	NN 4	MM 29
ZZ 14	YY 24	XX 5	WW 39	VV 25	UU 50	TT 21

AUGUST 19

NOTES

AUGUST 20

NOTES

		C 43	B 19	A 21		
J 47	I 6	H 44	G 29	F 14	E 7	D 5
Q 39	P 15	O 50	N 10	M 40	L 37	K 35
X 16	W 1	V 46	U 36	T 26	S 12	R 49
EE 45	DD 30	CC 24	BB 22	AA 8	Z 38	Y 33
LL 31	KK 13	JJ 41	II 52	HH 32	GG 17	FF 2
SS 9	RR 42	QQ 27	PP 20	OO 18	NN 3	MM 28
ZZ 51	YY 23	XX 4	WW 34	VV 48	UU 11	TT 25

AUGUST 21

NOTES

		C 42	B 18	A 25		
J 20	I 5	H 43	G 28	F 51	E 6	D 4
Q 34	P 14	O 11	N 9	M 7	L 36	K 39
X 15	W 50	V 45	U 35	T 21	S 47	R 46
EE 44	DD 29	CC 23	BB 26	AA 12	Z 49	Y 32
LL 30	KK 8	JJ 40	II 37	HH 31	GG 16	FF 1
SS 13	RR 41	QQ 52	PP 19	OO 17	NN 2	MM 27
ZZ 24	YY 22	XX 3	WW 38	VV 33	UU 10	TT 48

AUGUST 22

NOTES

AUGUST 23

NOTES

AUGUST 24

NOTES

C 7, B 15, A 32
J 17, I 2, H 40, G 37, F 22, E 3, D 1
Q 46, P 23, O 13, N 12, M 4, L 34, K 49
X 24, W 9, V 42, U 38, T 33, S 18, R 43
EE 41, DD 52, CC 21, BB 48, AA 19, Z 44, Y 29
LL 27, KK 20, JJ 5, II 39, HH 28, GG 51, FF 10
SS 47, RR 6, QQ 35, PP 16, OO 14, NN 11, MM 36
ZZ 26, YY 25, XX 50, WW 45, VV 30, UU 8, TT 31

AUGUST 25

NOTES

C 6, B 14, A 31
J 16, I 1, H 7, G 36, F 26, E 2, D 50
Q 45, P 22, O 8, N 47, M 3, L 38, K 46
X 23, W 13, V 41, U 49, T 32, S 17, R 42
EE 40, DD 37, CC 25, BB 33, AA 18, Z 43, Y 28
LL 52, KK 19, JJ 4, II 34, HH 27, GG 24, FF 9
SS 20, RR 5, QQ 39, PP 15, OO 51, NN 10, MM 35
ZZ 21, YY 48, XX 11, WW 44, VV 29, UU 12, TT 30

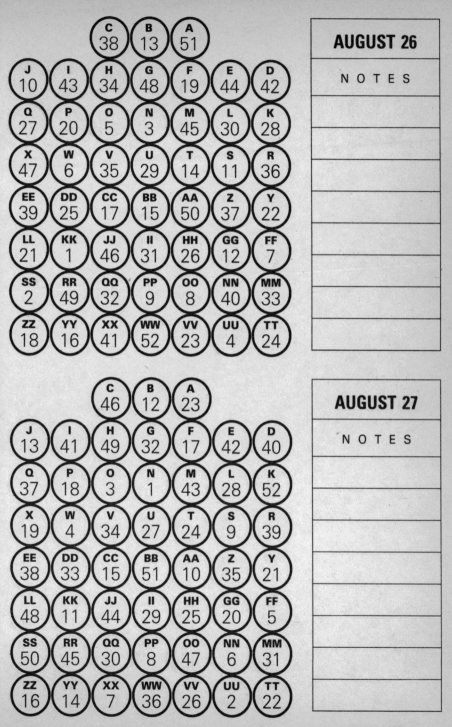

AUGUST 26

N O T E S

AUGUST 27

N O T E S

AUGUST 28

NOTES

		C 35	B 11	A 16		
J 1	I 46	H 36	G 26	F 12	E 49	D 45
Q 30	P 8	O 40	N 6	M 38	L 33	K 31
X 13	W 41	V 52	U 32	T 17	S 2	R 27
EE 37	DD 22	CC 20	BB 18	AA 3	Z 28	Y 51
LL 23	KK 4	JJ 34	II 48	HH 24	GG 9	FF 42
SS 5	RR 39	QQ 25	PP 50	OO 10	NN 43	MM 21
ZZ 47	YY 19	XX 44	WW 29	VV 14	UU 7	TT 15

AUGUST 29

NOTES

		C 39	B 10	A 15		
J 50	I 45	H 35	G 21	F 47	E 46	D 44
Q 29	P 12	O 7	N 5	M 49	L 32	K 30
X 8	W 40	V 37	U 31	T 16	S 1	R 52
EE 36	DD 26	CC 19	BB 17	AA 2	Z 27	Y 24
LL 22	KK 3	JJ 38	II 33	HH 23	GG 13	FF 41
SS 4	RR 34	QQ 48	PP 11	OO 9	NN 42	MM 25
ZZ 20	YY 18	XX 43	WW 28	VV 51	UU 6	TT 14

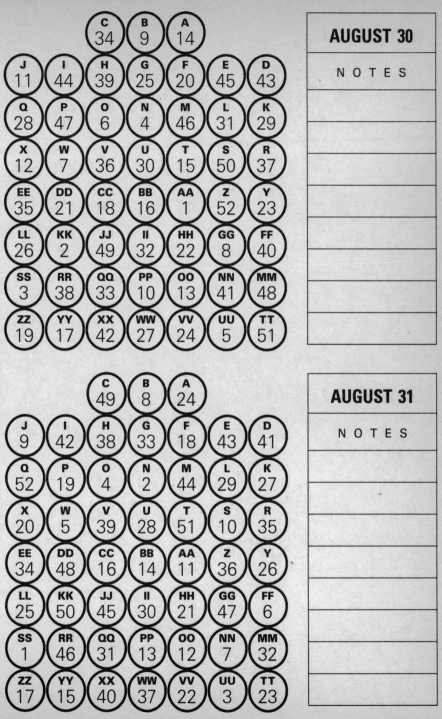

AUGUST 30

NOTES

		C 34	B 9	A 14		
J 11	I 44	H 39	G 25	F 20	E 45	D 43
Q 28	P 47	O 6	N 4	M 46	L 31	K 29
X 12	W 7	V 36	U 30	T 15	S 50	R 37
EE 35	DD 21	CC 18	BB 16	AA 1	Z 52	Y 23
LL 26	KK 2	JJ 49	II 32	HH 22	GG 8	FF 40
SS 3	RR 38	QQ 33	PP 10	OO 13	NN 41	MM 48
ZZ 19	YY 17	XX 42	WW 27	VV 24	UU 5	TT 51

AUGUST 31

NOTES

		C 49	B 8	A 24		
J 9	I 42	H 38	G 33	F 18	E 43	D 41
Q 52	P 19	O 4	N 2	M 44	L 29	K 27
X 20	W 5	V 39	U 28	T 51	S 10	R 35
EE 34	DD 48	CC 16	BB 14	AA 11	Z 36	Y 26
LL 25	KK 50	JJ 45	II 30	HH 21	GG 47	FF 6
SS 1	RR 46	QQ 31	PP 13	OO 12	NN 7	MM 32
ZZ 17	YY 15	XX 40	WW 37	VV 22	UU 3	TT 23

SEPTEMBER 1

NOTES

C 16	B 36	A 41

J 52	I 23	H 17	G 2	F 49	E 24	D 22
Q 8	P 38	O 33	N 31	M 51	L 10	K 13
X 34	W 48	V 19	U 9	T 42	S 27	R 20
EE 18	DD 3	CC 45	BB 43	AA 28	Z 47	Y 6
LL 4	KK 29	JJ 14	II 11	HH 5	GG 39	FF 25
SS 30	RR 15	QQ 50	PP 37	OO 35	NN 21	MM 1
ZZ 46	YY 44	XX 26	WW 12	VV 7	UU 32	TT 40

SEPTEMBER 2

NOTES

C 15	B 35	A 40

J 37	I 22	H 16	G 1	F 46	E 23	D 26
Q 12	P 49	O 32	N 30	M 24	L 9	K 8
X 38	W 33	V 18	U 13	T 41	S 52	R 19
EE 17	DD 2	CC 44	BB 42	AA 27	Z 20	Y 5
LL 3	KK 28	JJ 51	II 10	HH 4	GG 34	FF 48
SS 29	RR 14	QQ 11	PP 36	OO 39	NN 25	MM 50
ZZ 45	YY 43	XX 21	WW 47	VV 6	UU 31	TT 7

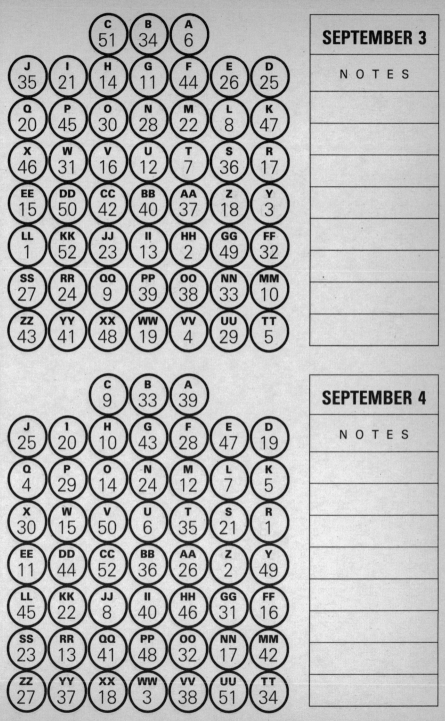

SEPTEMBER 3

NOTES

C	B	A
51	34	6

J	I	H	G	F	E	D
35	21	14	11	44	26	25

Q	P	O	N	M	L	K
20	45	30	28	22	8	47

X	W	V	U	T	S	R
46	31	16	12	7	36	17

EE	DD	CC	BB	AA	Z	Y
15	50	42	40	37	18	3

LL	KK	JJ	II	HH	GG	FF
1	52	23	13	2	49	32

SS	RR	QQ	PP	OO	NN	MM
27	24	9	39	38	33	10

ZZ	YY	XX	WW	VV	UU	TT
43	41	48	19	4	29	5

SEPTEMBER 4

NOTES

C	B	A
9	33	39

J	I	H	G	F	E	D
25	20	10	43	28	47	19

Q	P	O	N	M	L	K
4	29	14	24	12	7	5

X	W	V	U	T	S	R
30	15	50	6	35	21	1

EE	DD	CC	BB	AA	Z	Y
11	44	52	36	26	2	49

LL	KK	JJ	II	HH	GG	FF
45	22	8	40	46	31	16

SS	RR	QQ	PP	OO	NN	MM
23	13	41	48	32	17	42

ZZ	YY	XX	WW	VV	UU	TT
27	37	18	3	38	51	34

SEPTEMBER 5

NOTES

C 13	B 32	A 34

J 48	I 19	H 9	G 42	F 27	E 20	D 18
Q 3	P 28	O 51	N 23	M 47	L 6	K 4
X 29	W 14	V 11	U 5	T 39	S 25	R 50
EE 10	DD 43	CC 37	BB 35	AA 21	Z 1	Y 46
LL 44	KK 26	JJ 12	II 7	HH 45	GG 30	FF 15
SS 22	RR 8	QQ 40	PP 33	OO 31	NN 16	MM 41
ZZ 52	YY 36	XX 17	WW 2	VV 49	UU 24	TT 38

SEPTEMBER 6

NOTES

C 8	B 31	A 38

J 33	I 18	H 13	G 41	F 52	E 19	D 17
Q 2	P 27	O 24	N 22	M 20	L 5	K 3
X 28	W 51	V 10	U 4	T 34	S 48	R 11
EE 9	DD 42	CC 36	BB 39	AA 25	Z 50	Y 45
LL 43	KK 21	JJ 47	II 6	HH 44	GG 29	FF 14
SS 26	RR 12	QQ 7	PP 32	OO 30	NN 15	MM 40
ZZ 37	YY 35	XX 16	WW 1	VV 46	UU 23	TT 49

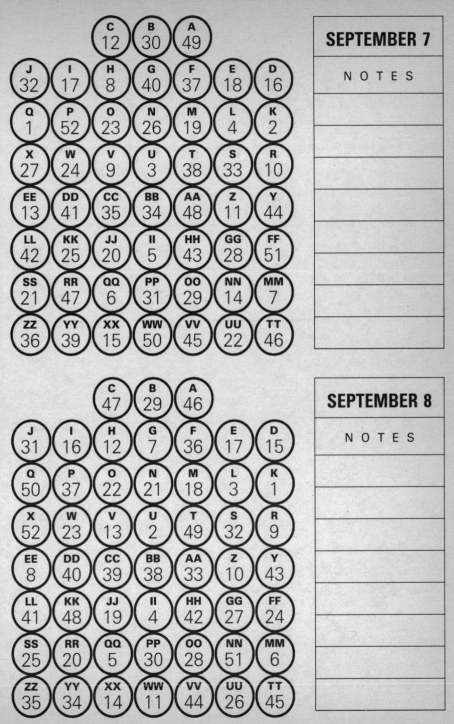

SEPTEMBER 7

NOTES

SEPTEMBER 8

NOTES

139

SEPTEMBER 9

NOTES

		C 20	B 28	A 45		
J 30	I 15	H 47	G 6	F 35	E 16	D 14
Q 11	P 36	O 26	N 25	M 17	L 2	K 50
X 37	W 22	V 8	U 1	T 46	S 31	R 13
EE 12	DD 7	CC 34	BB 49	AA 32	Z 9	Y 42
LL 40	KK 33	JJ 18	II 3	HH 41	GG 52	FF 23
SS 48	RR 19	QQ 4	PP 29	OO 27	NN 24	MM 5
ZZ 39	YY 38	XX 51	WW 10	VV 43	UU 21	TT 44

SEPTEMBER 10

NOTES

		C 19	B 27	A 44		
J 29	I 14	H 20	G 5	F 39	E 15	D 51
Q 10	P 35	O 21	N 48	M 16	L 1	K 11
X 36	W 26	V 12	U 50	T 45	S 30	R 8
EE 47	DD 6	CC 38	BB 46	AA 31	Z 13	Y 41
LL 7	KK 32	JJ 17	II 2	HH 40	GG 37	FF 22
SS 33	RR 18	QQ 3	PP 28	OO 52	NN 23	MM 4
ZZ 34	YY 49	XX 24	WW 9	VV 42	UU 25	TT 43

140

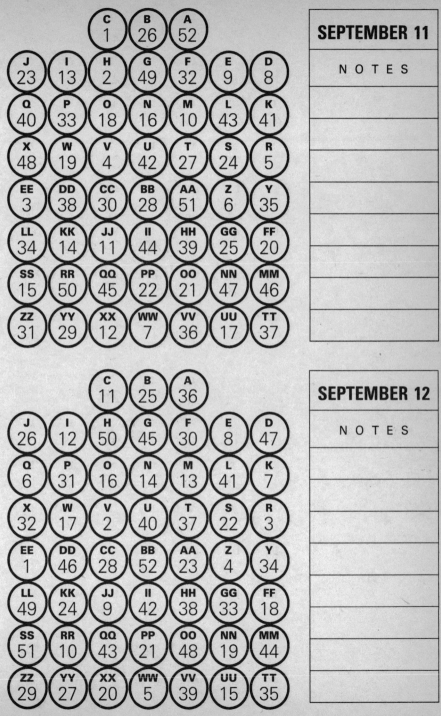

SEPTEMBER 11

NOTES

SEPTEMBER 12

NOTES

141

SEPTEMBER 13

NOTES

C 4 | B 24 | A 29

J 14 | I 11 | H 5 | G 39 | F 25 | E 50 | D 10

Q 43 | P 21 | O 47 | N 19 | M 1 | L 46 | K 44

X 26 | W 12 | V 7 | U 45 | T 30 | S 15 | R 40

EE 6 | DD 35 | CC 33 | BB 31 | AA 16 | Z 41 | Y 52

LL 36 | KK 17 | JJ 2 | II 49 | HH 37 | GG 22 | FF 8

SS 18 | RR 3 | QQ 38 | PP 51 | OO 23 | NN 13 | MM 34

ZZ 48 | YY 32 | XX 9 | WW 42 | VV 27 | UU 20 | TT 28

SEPTEMBER 14

NOTES

C 3 | B 23 | A 28

J 51 | I 10 | H 4 | G 34 | F 48 | E 11 | D 9

Q 42 | P 25 | O 20 | N 18 | M 50 | L 45 | K 43

X 21 | W 47 | V 6 | U 44 | T 29 | S 14 | R 7

EE 5 | DD 39 | CC 32 | BB 30 | AA 15 | Z 40 | Y 37

LL 35 | KK 16 | JJ 1 | II 46 | HH 36 | GG 26 | FF 12

SS 17 | RR 2 | QQ 49 | PP 24 | OO 22 | NN 8 | MM 38

ZZ 33 | YY 31 | XX 13 | WW 41 | VV 52 | UU 19 | TT 27

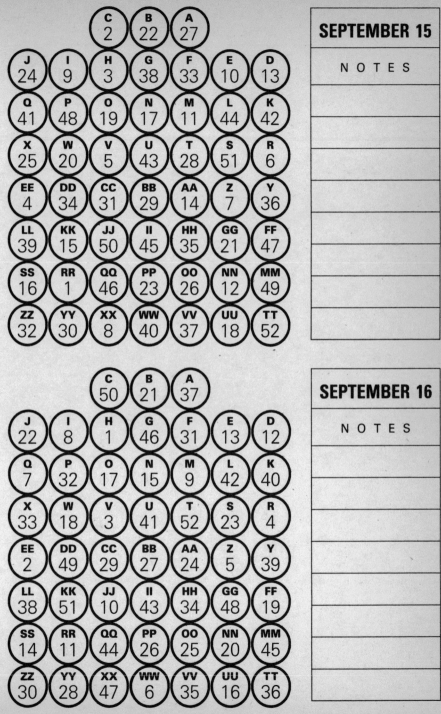

SEPTEMBER 15

NOTES

SEPTEMBER 16

NOTES

143

SEPTEMBER 17

NOTES

C	B	A
44	20	26

J	I	H	G	F	E	D
12	7	45	30	15	40	6

Q	P	O	N	M	L	K
35	16	1	11	41	52	36

X	W	V	U	T	S	R
17	2	49	37	22	8	38

EE	DD	CC	BB	AA	Z	Y
46	31	51	23	13	34	48

LL	KK	JJ	II	HH	GG	FF
32	9	42	27	33	18	3

SS	RR	QQ	PP	OO	NN	MM
10	43	28	47	19	4	29

ZZ	YY	XX	WW	VV	UU	TT
14	24	5	39	25	50	21

SEPTEMBER 18

NOTES

C	B	A
43	19	21

J	I	H	G	F	E	D
47	6	44	29	14	7	5

Q	P	O	N	M	L	K
39	15	50	10	40	37	35

X	W	V	U	T	S	R
16	1	46	36	26	12	49

EE	DD	CC	BB	AA	Z	Y
45	30	24	22	8	38	33

LL	KK	JJ	II	HH	GG	FF
31	13	41	52	32	17	2

SS	RR	QQ	PP	OO	NN	MM
9	42	27	20	18	3	28

ZZ	YY	XX	WW	VV	UU	TT
51	23	4	34	48	11	25

SEPTEMBER 19

NOTES

SEPTEMBER 20

NOTES

145

SEPTEMBER 21

NOTES

		C 40	B 16	A 33		
J 18	I 3	H 41	G 52	F 23	E 4	D 2
Q 49	P 24	O 9	N 8	M 5	L 39	K 38
X 51	W 10	V 43	U 34	T 48	S 19	R 44
EE 42	DD 27	CC 26	BB 25	AA 20	Z 45	Y 30
LL 28	KK 47	JJ 6	II 35	HH 29	GG 14	FF 11
SS 12	RR 7	QQ 36	PP 17	OO 15	NN 50	MM 37
ZZ 22	YY 21	XX 1	WW 46	VV 31	UU 13	TT 32

SEPTEMBER 22

NOTES

		C 7	B 15	A 32		
J 17	I 2	H 40	G 37	F 22	E 3	D 1
Q 46	P 23	O 13	N 12	M 4	L 34	K 49
X 24	W 9	V 42	U 38	T 33	S 18	R 43
EE 41	DD 52	CC 21	BB 48	AA 19	Z 44	Y 29
LL 27	KK 20	JJ 5	II 39	HH 28	GG 51	FF 10
SS 47	RR 6	QQ 35	PP 16	OO 14	NN 11	MM 36
ZZ 26	YY 25	XX 50	WW 45	VV 30	UU 8	TT 31

SEPTEMBER 23

NOTES

SEPTEMBER 24

NOTES

SEPTEMBER 25

NOTES

C 46 · B 12 · A 23

J 13 · I 41 · H 49 · G 32 · F 17 · E 42 · D 40

Q 37 · P 18 · O 3 · N 1 · M 43 · L 28 · K 52

X 19 · W 4 · V 34 · U 27 · T 24 · S 9 · R 39

EE 38 · DD 33 · CC 15 · BB 51 · AA 10 · Z 35 · Y 21

LL 48 · KK 11 · JJ 44 · II 29 · HH 25 · GG 20 · FF 5

SS 50 · RR 45 · QQ 30 · PP 8 · OO 47 · NN 6 · MM 31

ZZ 16 · YY 14 · XX 7 · WW 36 · VV 26 · UU 2 · TT 22

SEPTEMBER 26

NOTES

C 35 · B 11 · A 16

J 1 · I 46 · H 36 · G 26 · F 12 · E 49 · D 45

Q 30 · P 8 · O 40 · N 6 · M 38 · L 33 · K 31

X 13 · W 41 · V 52 · U 32 · T 17 · S 2 · R 27

EE 37 · DD 22 · CC 20 · BB 18 · AA 3 · Z 28 · Y 51

LL 23 · KK 4 · JJ 34 · II 48 · HH 24 · GG 9 · FF 42

SS 5 · RR 39 · QQ 25 · PP 50 · OO 10 · NN 43 · MM 21

ZZ 47 · YY 19 · XX 44 · WW 29 · VV 14 · UU 7 · TT 15

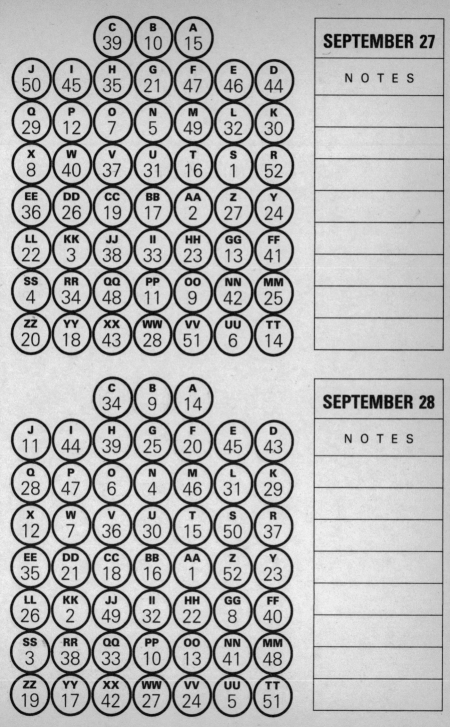

		C 39	B 10	A 15		
J 50	I 45	H 35	G 21	F 47	E 46	D 44
Q 29	P 12	O 7	N 5	M 49	L 32	K 30
X 8	W 40	V 37	U 31	T 16	S 1	R 52
EE 36	DD 26	CC 19	BB 17	AA 2	Z 27	Y 24
LL 22	KK 3	JJ 38	II 33	HH 23	GG 13	FF 41
SS 4	RR 34	QQ 48	PP 11	OO 9	NN 42	MM 25
ZZ 20	YY 18	XX 43	WW 28	VV 51	UU 6	TT 14

SEPTEMBER 27

NOTES

		C 34	B 9	A 14		
J 11	I 44	H 39	G 25	F 20	E 45	D 43
Q 28	P 47	O 6	N 4	M 46	L 31	K 29
X 12	W 7	V 36	U 30	T 15	S 50	R 37
EE 35	DD 21	CC 18	BB 16	AA 1	Z 52	Y 23
LL 26	KK 2	JJ 49	II 32	HH 22	GG 8	FF 40
SS 3	RR 38	QQ 33	PP 10	OO 13	NN 41	MM 48
ZZ 19	YY 17	XX 42	WW 27	VV 24	UU 5	TT 51

SEPTEMBER 28

NOTES

149

SEPTEMBER 29

NOTES

C 49	B 8	A 24

J 9	I 42	H 38	G 33	F 18	E 43	D 41
Q 52	P 19	O 4	N 2	M 44	L 29	K 27
X 20	W 5	V 39	U 28	T 51	S 10	R 35
EE 34	DD 48	CC 16	BB 14	AA 11	Z 36	Y 26
LL 25	KK 50	JJ 45	II 30	HH 21	GG 47	FF 6
SS 1	RR 46	QQ 31	PP 13	OO 12	NN 7	MM 32
ZZ 17	YY 15	XX 40	WW 37	VV 22	UU 3	TT 23

SEPTEMBER 30

NOTES

C 31	B 7	A 13

J 41	I 52	H 32	G 17	F 2	E 27	D 37
Q 22	P 3	O 38	N 46	M 28	L 51	K 23
X 4	W 34	V 48	U 24	T 9	S 42	R 25
EE 33	DD 18	CC 50	BB 10	AA 43	Z 21	Y 47
LL 19	KK 44	JJ 29	II 14	HH 20	GG 5	FF 39
SS 45	RR 30	QQ 15	PP 40	OO 6	NN 35	MM 16
ZZ 1	YY 11	XX 36	WW 26	VV 12	UU 49	TT 8

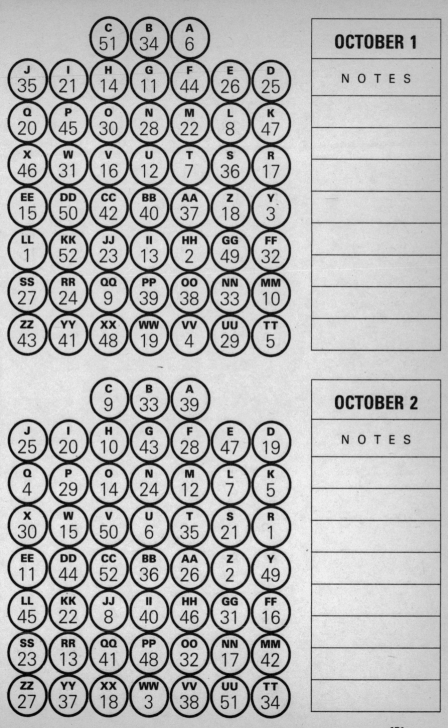

OCTOBER 1

NOTES

OCTOBER 2

NOTES

OCTOBER 3

NOTES

C 13 · B 32 · A 34

J 48 · I 19 · H 9 · G 42 · F 27 · E 20 · D 18

Q 3 · P 28 · O 51 · N 23 · M 47 · L 6 · K 4

X 29 · W 14 · V 11 · U 5 · T 39 · S 25 · R 50

EE 10 · DD 43 · CC 37 · BB 35 · AA 21 · Z 1 · Y 46

LL 44 · KK 26 · JJ 12 · II 7 · HH 45 · GG 30 · FF 15

SS 22 · RR 8 · QQ 40 · PP 33 · OO 31 · NN 16 · MM 41

ZZ 52 · YY 36 · XX 17 · WW 2 · VV 49 · UU 24 · TT 38

OCTOBER 4

NOTES

C 8 · B 31 · A 38

J 33 · I 18 · H 13 · G 41 · F 52 · E 19 · D 17

Q 2 · P 27 · O 24 · N 22 · M 20 · L 5 · K 3

X 28 · W 51 · V 10 · U 4 · T 34 · S 48 · R 11

EE 9 · DD 42 · CC 36 · BB 39 · AA 25 · Z 50 · Y 45

LL 43 · KK 21 · JJ 47 · II 6 · HH 44 · GG 29 · FF 14

SS 26 · RR 12 · QQ 7 · PP 32 · OO 30 · NN 15 · MM 40

ZZ 37 · YY 35 · XX 16 · WW 1 · VV 46 · UU 23 · TT 49

OCTOBER 5

NOTES

OCTOBER 6

NOTES

153

OCTOBER 7

NOTES

		C 20	B 28	A 45		
J 30	I 15	H 47	G 6	F 35	E 16	D 14
Q 11	P 36	O 26	N 25	M 17	L 2	K 50
X 37	W 22	V 8	U 1	T 46	S 31	R 13
EE 12	DD 7	CC 34	BB 49	AA 32	Z 9	Y 42
LL 40	KK 33	JJ 18	II 3	HH 41	GG 52	FF 23
SS 48	RR 19	QQ 4	PP 29	OO 27	NN 24	MM 5
ZZ 39	YY 38	XX 51	WW 10	VV 43	UU 21	TT 44

OCTOBER 8

NOTES

		C 19	B 27	A 44		
J 29	I 14	H 20	G 5	F 39	E 15	D 51
Q 10	P 35	O 21	N 48	M 16	L 1	K 11
X 36	W 26	V 12	U 50	T 45	S 30	R 8
EE 47	DD 6	CC 38	BB 46	AA 31	Z 13	Y 41
LL 7	KK 32	JJ 17	II 2	HH 40	GG 37	FF 22
SS 33	RR 18	QQ 3	PP 28	OO 52	NN 23	MM 4
ZZ 34	YY 49	XX 24	WW 9	VV 42	UU 25	TT 43

154

OCTOBER 9

NOTES

OCTOBER 10

NOTES

155

OCTOBER 11

NOTES

		C 4	B 24	A 29		
J 14	I 11	H 5	G 39	F 25	E 50	D 10
Q 43	P 21	O 47	N 19	M 1	L 46	K 44
X 26	W 12	V 7	U 45	T 30	S 15	R 40
EE 6	DD 35	CC 33	BB 31	AA 16	Z 41	Y 52
LL 36	KK 17	JJ 2	II 49	HH 37	GG 22	FF 8
SS 18	RR 3	QQ 38	PP 51	OO 23	NN 13	MM 34
ZZ 48	YY 32	XX 9	WW 42	VV 27	UU 20	TT 28

OCTOBER 12

NOTES

		C 3	B 23	A 28		
J 51	I 10	H 4	G 34	F 48	E 11	D 9
Q 42	P 25	O 20	N 18	M 50	L 45	K 43
X 21	W 47	V 6	U 44	T 29	S 14	R 7
EE 5	DD 39	CC 32	BB 30	AA 15	Z 40	Y 37
LL 35	KK 16	JJ 1	II 46	HH 36	GG 26	FF 12
SS 17	RR 2	QQ 49	PP 24	OO 22	NN 8	MM 38
ZZ 33	YY 31	XX 13	WW 41	VV 52	UU 19	TT 27

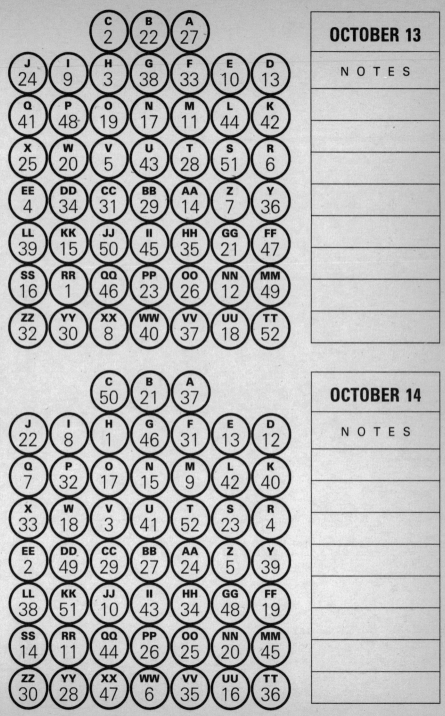

OCTOBER 13

NOTES

OCTOBER 14

NOTES

157

OCTOBER 15

NOTES

C 44	B 20	A 26

J 12	I 7	H 45	G 30	F 15	E 40	D 6
Q 35	P 16	O 1	N 11	M 41	L 52	K 36
X 17	W 2	V 49	U 37	T 22	S 8	R 38
EE 46	DD 31	CC 51	BB 23	AA 13	Z 34	Y 48
LL 32	KK 9	JJ 42	II 27	HH 33	GG 18	FF 3
SS 10	RR 43	QQ 28	PP 47	OO 19	NN 4	MM 29
ZZ 14	YY 24	XX 5	WW 39	VV 25	UU 50	TT 21

OCTOBER 16

NOTES

C 43	B 19	A 21

J 47	I 6	H 44	G 29	F 14	E 7	D 5
Q 39	P 15	O 50	N 10	M 40	L 37	K 35
X 16	W 1	V 46	U 36	T 26	S 12	R 49
EE 45	DD 30	CC 24	BB 22	AA 8	Z 38	Y 33
LL 31	KK 13	JJ 41	II 52	HH 32	GG 17	FF 2
SS 9	RR 42	QQ 27	PP 20	OO 18	NN 3	MM 28
ZZ 51	YY 23	XX 4	WW 34	VV 48	UU 11	TT 25

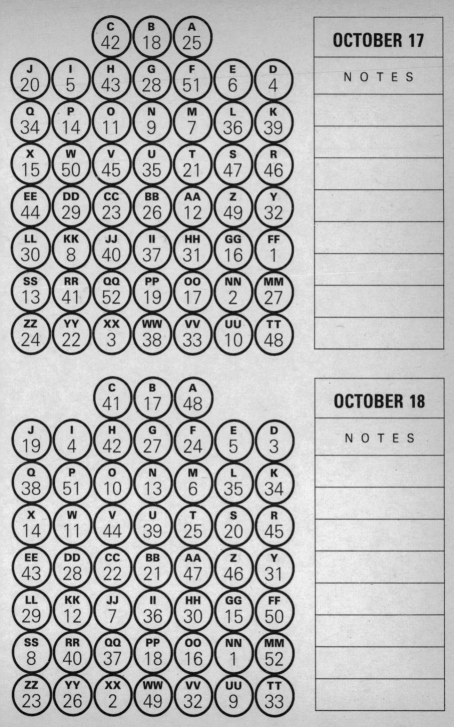

OCTOBER 17

NOTES

OCTOBER 18

NOTES

159

OCTOBER 19

NOTES

		C 40	B 16	A 33		
J 18	I 3	H 41	G 52	F 23	E 4	D 2
Q 49	P 24	O 9	N 8	M 5	L 39	K 38
X 51	W 10	V 43	U 34	T 48	S 19	R 44
EE 42	DD 27	CC 26	BB 25	AA 20	Z 45	Y 30
LL 28	KK 47	JJ 6	II 35	HH 29	GG 14	FF 11
SS 12	RR 7	QQ 36	PP 17	OO 15	NN 50	MM 37
ZZ 22	YY 21	XX 1	WW 46	VV 31	UU 13	TT 32

OCTOBER 20

NOTES

.

		C 7	B 15	A 32		
J 17	I 2	H 40	G 37	F 22	E 3	D 1
Q 46	P 23	O 13	N 12	M 4	L 34	K 49
X 24	W 9	V 42	U 38	T 33	S 18	R 43
EE 41	DD 52	CC 21	BB 48	AA 19	Z 44	Y 29
LL 27	KK 20	JJ 5	II 39	HH 28	GG 51	FF 10
SS 47	RR 6	QQ 35	PP 16	OO 14	NN 11	MM 36
ZZ 26	YY 25	XX 50	WW 45	VV 30	UU 8	TT 31

OCTOBER 21

NOTES

OCTOBER 22

NOTES

161

OCTOBER 23

NOTES

			A 23	B 12	C 46

- C 46, B 12, A 23
- J 13, I 41, H 49, G 32, F 17, E 42, D 40
- Q 37, P 18, O 3, N 1, M 43, L 28, K 52
- X 19, W 4, V 34, U 27, T 24, S 9, R 39
- EE 38, DD 33, CC 15, BB 51, AA 10, Z 35, Y 21
- LL 48, KK 11, JJ 44, II 29, HH 25, GG 20, FF 5
- SS 50, RR 45, QQ 30, PP 8, OO 47, NN 6, MM 31
- ZZ 16, YY 14, XX 7, WW 36, VV 26, UU 2, TT 22

OCTOBER 24

NOTES

- C 35, B 11, A 16
- J 1, I 46, H 36, G 26, F 12, E 49, D 45
- Q 30, P 8, O 40, N 6, M 38, L 33, K 31
- X 13, W 41, V 52, U 32, T 17, S 2, R 27
- EE 37, DD 22, CC 20, BB 18, AA 3, Z 28, Y 51
- LL 23, KK 4, JJ 34, II 48, HH 24, GG 9, FF 42
- SS 5, RR 39, QQ 25, PP 50, OO 10, NN 43, MM 21
- ZZ 47, YY 19, XX 44, WW 29, VV 14, UU 7, TT 15

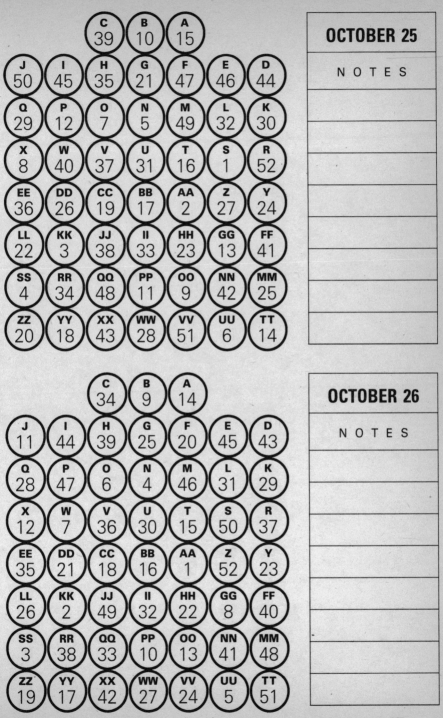

OCTOBER 25

NOTES

OCTOBER 26

NOTES

OCTOBER 27

NOTES

		C 49	B 8	A 24		
J 9	I 42	H 38	G 33	F 18	E 43	D 41
Q 52	P 19	O 4	N 2	M 44	L 29	K 27
X 20	W 5	V 39	U 28	T 51	S 10	R 35
EE 34	DD 48	CC 16	BB 14	AA 11	Z 36	Y 26
LL 25	KK 50	JJ 45	II 30	HH 21	GG 47	FF 6
SS 1	RR 46	QQ 31	PP 13	OO 12	NN 7	MM 32
ZZ 17	YY 15	XX 40	WW 37	VV 22	UU 3	TT 23

OCTOBER 28

NOTES

		C 31	B 7	A 13		
J 41	I 52	H 32	G 17	F 2	E 27	D 37
Q 22	P 3	O 38	N 46	M 28	L 51	K 23
X 4	W 34	V 48	U 24	T 9	S 42	R 25
EE 33	DD 18	CC 50	BB 10	AA 43	Z 21	Y 47
LL 19	KK 44	JJ 29	II 14	HH 20	GG 5	FF 39
SS 45	RR 30	QQ 15	PP 40	OO 6	NN 35	MM 16
ZZ 1	YY 11	XX 36	WW 26	VV 12	UU 49	TT 8

OCTOBER 29

NOTES

OCTOBER 30

NOTES

165

OCTOBER 31

NOTES

		C 28	B 4	A 47		
J 6	I 35	H 29	G 14	F 11	E 36	D 39
Q 25	P 50	O 45	N 43	M 37	L 22	K 21
X 1	W 46	V 31	U 26	T 12	S 7	R 32
EE 30	DD 15	CC 9	BB 8	AA 40	Z 33	Y 18
LL 16	KK 41	JJ 52	II 23	HH 17	GG 2	FF 49
SS 42	RR 27	QQ 24	PP 5	OO 3	NN 38	MM 51
ZZ 10	YY 13	XX 34	WW 48	VV 19	UU 44	TT 20

NOVEMBER 1

NOTES

		C 13	B 32	A 34		
J 48	I 19	H 9	G 42	F 27	E 20	D 18
Q 3	P 28	O 51	N 23	M 47	L 6	K 4
X 29	W 14	V 11	U 5	T 39	S 25	R 50
EE 10	DD 43	CC 37	BB 35	AA 21	Z 1	Y 46
LL 44	KK 26	JJ 12	II 7	HH 45	GG 30	FF 15
SS 22	RR 8	QQ 40	PP 33	OO 31	NN 16	MM 41
ZZ 52	YY 36	XX 17	WW 2	VV 49	UU 24	TT 38

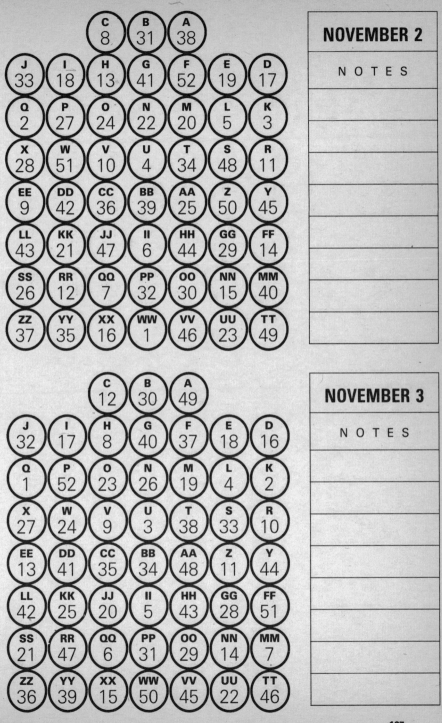

NOVEMBER 2

NOTES

NOVEMBER 3

NOTES

NOVEMBER 4

NOTES

C 47	B 29	A 46

J 31	I 16	H 12	G 7	F 36	E 17	D 15
Q 50	P 37	O 22	N 21	M 18	L 3	K 1
X 52	W 23	V 13	U 2	T 49	S 32	R 9
EE 8	DD 40	CC 39	BB 38	AA 33	Z 10	Y 43
LL 41	KK 48	JJ 19	II 4	HH 42	GG 27	FF 24
SS 25	RR 20	QQ 5	PP 30	OO 28	NN 51	MM 6
ZZ 35	YY 34	XX 14	WW 11	VV 44	UU 26	TT 45

NOVEMBER 5

NOTES

C 20	B 28	A 45

J 30	I 15	H 47	G 6	F 35	E 16	D 14
Q 11	P 36	O 26	N 25	M 17	L 2	K 50
X 37	W 22	V 8	U 1	T 46	S 31	R 13
EE 12	DD 7	CC 34	BB 49	AA 32	Z 9	Y 42
LL 40	KK 33	JJ 18	II 3	HH 41	GG 52	FF 23
SS 48	RR 19	QQ 4	PP 29	OO 27	NN 24	MM 5
ZZ 39	YY 38	XX 51	WW 10	VV 43	UU 21	TT 44

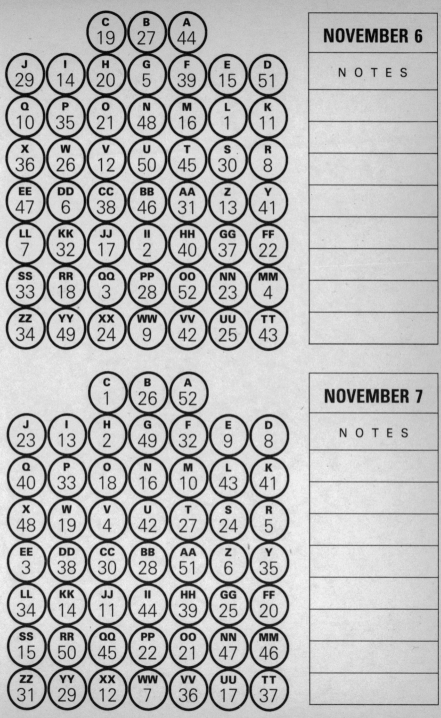

NOVEMBER 8

NOTES

			C 11	B 25	A 36	
J 26	I 12	H 50	G 45	F 30	E 8	D 47
Q 6	P 31	O 16	N 14	M 13	L 41	K 7
X 32	W 17	V 2	U 40	T 37	S 22	R 3
EE 1	DD 46	CC 28	BB 52	AA 23	Z 4	Y 34
LL 49	KK 24	JJ 9	II 42	HH 38	GG 33	FF 18
SS 51	RR 10	QQ 43	PP 21	OO 48	NN 19	MM 44
ZZ 29	YY 27	XX 20	WW 5	VV 39	UU 15	TT 35

NOVEMBER 9

NOTES

			C 4	B 24	A 29	
J 14	I 11	H 5	G 39	F 25	E 50	D 10
Q 43	P 21	O 47	N 19	M 1	L 46	K 44
X 26	W 12	V 7	U 45	T 30	S 15	R 40
EE 6	DD 35	CC 33	BB 31	AA 16	Z 41	Y 52
LL 36	KK 17	JJ 2	II 49	HH 37	GG 22	FF 8
SS 18	RR 3	QQ 38	PP 51	OO 23	NN 13	MM 34
ZZ 48	YY 32	XX 9	WW 42	VV 27	UU 20	TT 28

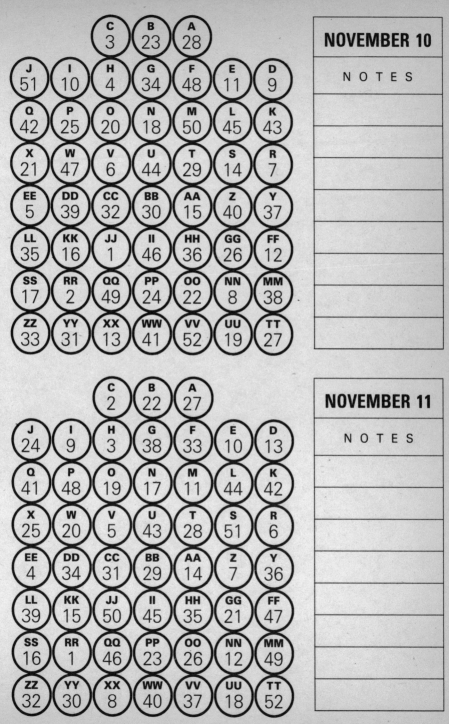

NOVEMBER 12

NOTES

		C 50	B 21	A 37	
J 22	I 8	H 1	G 46	F 31	E 13	D 12
Q 7	P 32	O 17	N 15	M 9	L 42	K 40
X 33	W 18	V 3	U 41	T 52	S 23	R 4
EE 2	DD 49	CC 29	BB 27	AA 24	Z 5	Y 39
LL 38	KK 51	JJ 10	II 43	HH 34	GG 48	FF 19
SS 14	RR 11	QQ 44	PP 26	OO 25	NN 20	MM 45
ZZ 30	YY 28	XX 47	WW 6	VV 35	UU 16	TT 36

NOVEMBER 13

NOTES

		C 44	B 20	A 26	
J 12	I 7	H 45	G 30	F 15	E 40	D 6
Q 35	P 16	O 1	N 11	M 41	L 52	K 36
X 17	W 2	V 49	U 37	T 22	S 8	R 38
EE 46	DD 31	CC 51	BB 23	AA 13	Z 34	Y 48
LL 32	KK 9	JJ 42	II 27	HH 33	GG 18	FF 3
SS 10	RR 43	QQ 28	PP 47	OO 19	NN 4	MM 29
ZZ 14	YY 24	XX 5	WW 39	VV 25	UU 50	TT 21

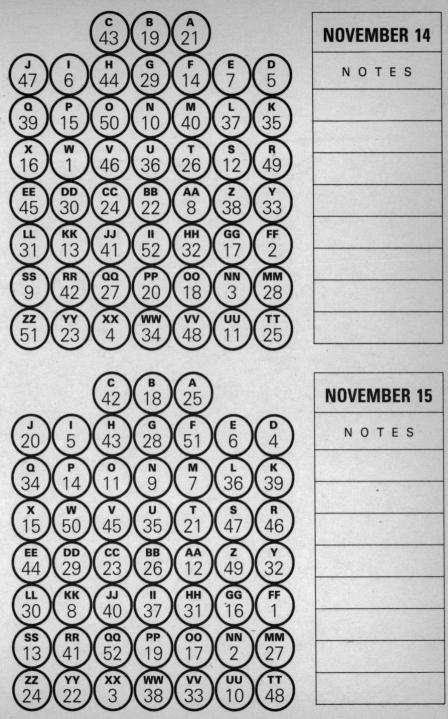

NOVEMBER 14

NOTES

NOVEMBER 15

NOTES

173

NOVEMBER 16

NOTES

C 41	B 17	A 48

J	I	H	G	F	E	D
19	4	42	27	24	5	3

Q	P	O	N	M	L	K
38	51	10	13	6	35	34

X	W	V	U	T	S	R
14	11	44	39	25	20	45

EE	DD	CC	BB	AA	Z	Y
43	28	22	21	47	46	31

LL	KK	JJ	II	HH	GG	FF
29	12	7	36	30	15	50

SS	RR	QQ	PP	OO	NN	MM
8	40	37	18	16	1	52

ZZ	YY	XX	WW	VV	UU	TT
23	26	2	49	32	9	33

NOVEMBER 17

NOTES

C 40	B 16	A 33

J	I	H	G	F	E	D
18	3	41	52	23	4	2

Q	P	O	N	M	L	K
49	24	9	8	5	39	38

X	W	V	U	T	S	R
51	10	43	34	48	19	44

EE	DD	CC	BB	AA	Z	Y
42	27	26	25	20	45	30

LL	KK	JJ	II	HH	GG	FF
28	47	6	35	29	14	11

SS	RR	QQ	PP	OO	NN	MM
12	7	36	17	15	50	37

ZZ	YY	XX	WW	VV	UU	TT
22	21	1	46	31	13	32

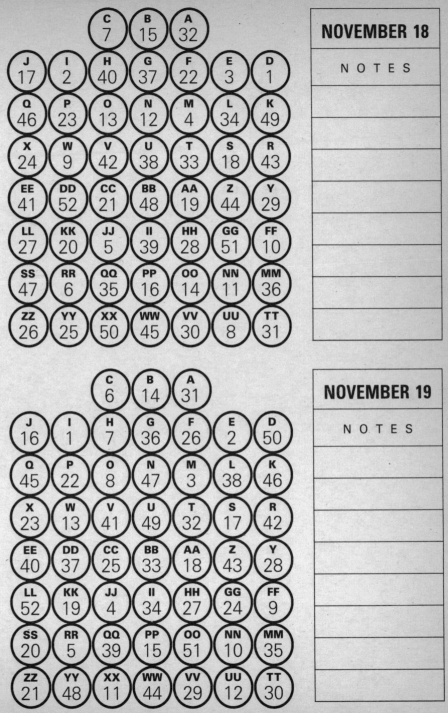

NOVEMBER 18

NOTES

NOVEMBER 19

NOTES

NOVEMBER 20

NOTES

| C 38 | B 13 | A 51 |

J 10	I 43	H 34	G 48	F 19	E 44	D 42
Q 27	P 20	O 5	N 3	M 45	L 30	K 28
X 47	W 6	V 35	U 29	T 14	S 11	R 36
EE 39	DD 25	CC 17	BB 15	AA 50	Z 37	Y 22
LL 21	KK 1	JJ 46	II 31	HH 26	GG 12	FF 7
SS 2	RR 49	QQ 32	PP 9	OO 8	NN 40	MM 33
ZZ 18	YY 16	XX 41	WW 52	VV 23	UU 4	TT 24

NOVEMBER 21

NOTES

| C 46 | B 12 | A 23 |

J 13	I 41	H 49	G 32	F 17	E 42	D 40
Q 37	P 18	O 3	N 1	M 43	L 28	K 52
X 19	W 4	V 34	U 27	T 24	S 9	R 39
EE 38	DD 33	CC 15	BB 51	AA 10	Z 35	Y 21
LL 48	KK 11	JJ 44	II 29	HH 25	GG 20	FF 5
SS 50	RR 45	QQ 30	PP 8	OO 47	NN 6	MM 31
ZZ 16	YY 14	XX 7	WW 36	VV 26	UU 2	TT 22

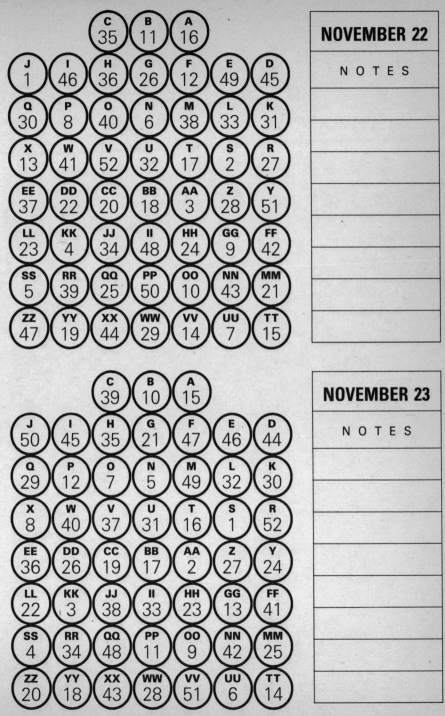

NOVEMBER 24

NOTES

	C 34	B 9	A 14

J 11	I 44	H 39	G 25	F 20	E 45	D 43
Q 28	P 47	O 6	N 4	M 46	L 31	K 29
X 12	W 7	V 36	U 30	T 15	S 50	R 37
EE 35	DD 21	CC 18	BB 16	AA 1	Z 52	Y 23
LL 26	KK 2	JJ 49	II 32	HH 22	GG 8	FF 40
SS 3	RR 38	QQ 33	PP 10	OO 13	NN 41	MM 48
ZZ 19	YY 17	XX 42	WW 27	VV 24	UU 5	TT 51

NOVEMBER 25

NOTES

	C 49	B 8	A 24

J 9	I 42	H 38	G 33	F 18	E 43	D 41
Q 52	P 19	O 4	N 2	M 44	L 29	K 27
X 20	W 5	V 39	U 28	T 51	S 10	R 35
EE 34	DD 48	CC 16	BB 14	AA 11	Z 36	Y 26
LL 25	KK 50	JJ 45	II 30	HH 21	GG 47	FF 6
SS 1	RR 46	QQ 31	PP 13	OO 12	NN 7	MM 32
ZZ 17	YY 15	XX 40	WW 37	VV 22	UU 3	TT 23

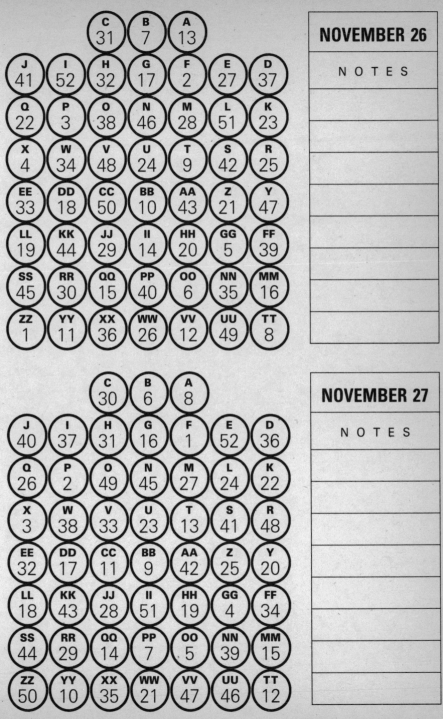

NOVEMBER 28

NOTES

C 29 B 5 A 12

J 7 I 36 H 30 G 15 F 50 E 37 D 35

Q 21 P 1 O 46 N 44 M 52 L 23 K 26

X 2 W 49 V 32 U 22 T 8 S 40 R 33

EE 31 DD 16 CC 10 BB 13 AA 41 Z 48 Y 19

LL 17 KK 42 JJ 27 II 24 HH 18 GG 3 FF 38

SS 43 RR 28 QQ 51 PP 6 OO 4 NN 34 MM 14

ZZ 11 YY 9 XX 39 WW 25 VV 20 UU 45 TT 47

NOVEMBER 29

NOTES

C 28 B 4 A 47

J 6 I 35 H 29 G 14 F 11 E 36 D 39

Q 25 P 50 O 45 N 43 M 37 L 22 K 21

X 1 W 46 V 31 U 26 T 12 S 7 R 32

EE 30 DD 15 CC 9 BB 8 AA 40 Z 33 Y 18

LL 16 KK 41 JJ 52 II 23 HH 17 GG 2 FF 49

SS 42 RR 27 QQ 24 PP 5 OO 3 NN 38 MM 51

ZZ 10 YY 13 XX 34 WW 48 VV 19 UU 44 TT 20

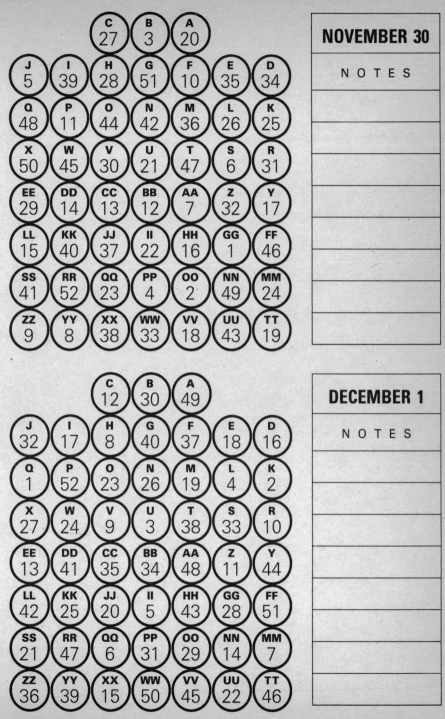

NOVEMBER 30

N O T E S

DECEMBER 1

N O T E S

181

DECEMBER 2

NOTES

	C 47	B 29	A 46

J 31	I 16	H 12	G 7	F 36	E 17	D 15
Q 50	P 37	O 22	N 21	M 18	L 3	K 1
X 52	W 23	V 13	U 2	T 49	S 32	R 9
EE 8	DD 40	CC 39	BB 38	AA 33	Z 10	Y 43
LL 41	KK 48	JJ 19	II 4	HH 42	GG 27	FF 24
SS 25	RR 20	QQ 5	PP 30	OO 28	NN 51	MM 6
ZZ 35	YY 34	XX 14	WW 11	VV 44	UU 26	TT 45

DECEMBER 3

NOTES

	C 20	B 28	A 45

J 30	I 15	H 47	G 6	F 35	E 16	D 14
Q 11	P 36	O 26	N 25	M 17	L 2	K 50
X 37	W 22	V 8	U 1	T 46	S 31	R 13
EE 12	DD 7	CC 34	BB 49	AA 32	Z 9	Y 42
LL 40	KK 33	JJ 18	II 3	HH 41	GG 52	FF 23
SS 48	RR 19	QQ 4	PP 29	OO 27	NN 24	MM 5
ZZ 39	YY 38	XX 51	WW 10	VV 43	UU 21	TT 44

DECEMBER 4

NOTES

DECEMBER 5

NOTES

DECEMBER 6

NOTES

C 11	B 25	A 36

J 26	I 12	H 50	G 45	F 30	E 8	D 47
Q 6	P 31	O 16	N 14	M 13	L 41	K 7
X 32	W 17	V 2	U 40	T 37	S 22	R 3
EE 1	DD 46	CC 28	BB 52	AA 23	Z 4	Y 34
LL 49	KK 24	JJ 9	II 42	HH 38	GG 33	FF 18
SS 51	RR 10	QQ 43	PP 21	OO 48	NN 19	MM 44
ZZ 29	YY 27	XX 20	WW 5	VV 39	UU 15	TT 35

DECEMBER 7

NOTES

C 4	B 24	A 29

J 14	I 11	H 5	G 39	F 25	E 50	D 10
Q 43	P 21	O 47	N 19	M 1	L 46	K 44
X 26	W 12	V 7	U 45	T 30	S 15	R 40
EE 6	DD 35	CC 33	BB 31	AA 16	Z 41	Y 52
LL 36	KK 17	JJ 2	II 49	HH 37	GG 22	FF 8
SS 18	RR 3	QQ 38	PP 51	OO 23	NN 13	MM 34
ZZ 48	YY 32	XX 9	WW 42	VV 27	UU 20	TT 28

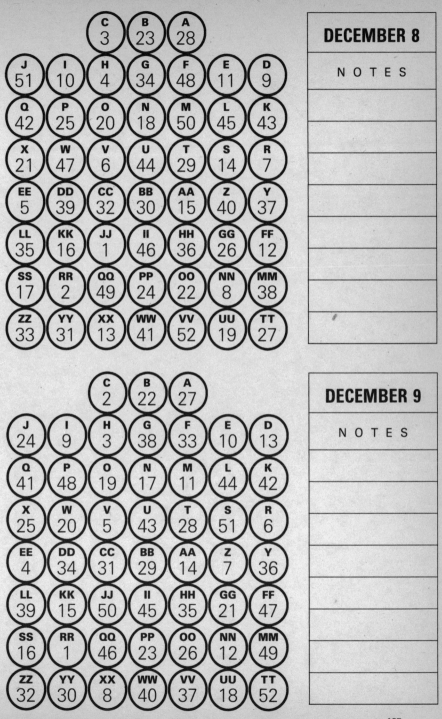

DECEMBER 8

NOTES

DECEMBER 9

NOTES

185

DECEMBER 10

NOTES

C 50 · B 21 · A 37

J 22 · I 8 · H 1 · G 46 · F 31 · E 13 · D 12

Q 7 · P 32 · O 17 · N 15 · M 9 · L 42 · K 40

X 33 · W 18 · V 3 · U 41 · T 52 · S 23 · R 4

EE 2 · DD 49 · CC 29 · BB 27 · AA 24 · Z 5 · Y 39

LL 38 · KK 51 · JJ 10 · II 43 · HH 34 · GG 48 · FF 19

SS 14 · RR 11 · QQ 44 · PP 26 · OO 25 · NN 20 · MM 45

ZZ 30 · YY 28 · XX 47 · WW 6 · VV 35 · UU 16 · TT 36

DECEMBER 11

NOTES

C 44 · B 20 · A 26

J 12 · I 7 · H 45 · G 30 · F 15 · E 40 · D 6

Q 35 · P 16 · O 1 · N 11 · M 41 · L 52 · K 36

X 17 · W 2 · V 49 · U 37 · T 22 · S 8 · R 38

EE 46 · DD 31 · CC 51 · BB 23 · AA 13 · Z 34 · Y 48

LL 32 · KK 9 · JJ 42 · II 27 · HH 33 · GG 18 · FF 3

SS 10 · RR 43 · QQ 28 · PP 47 · OO 19 · NN 4 · MM 29

ZZ 14 · YY 24 · XX 5 · WW 39 · VV 25 · UU 50 · TT 21

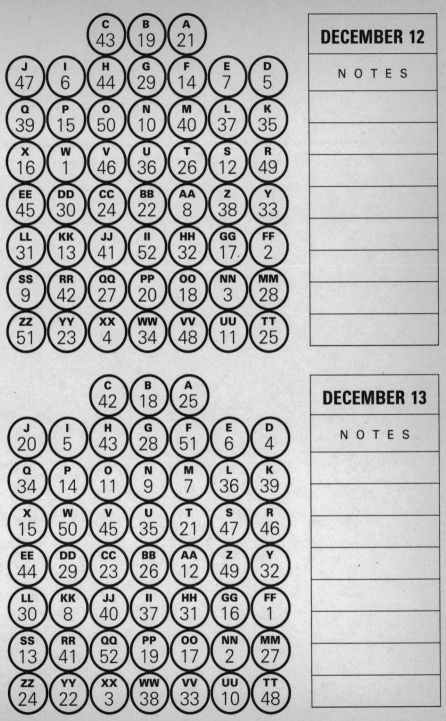

NOTES

DECEMBER 13

NOTES

187

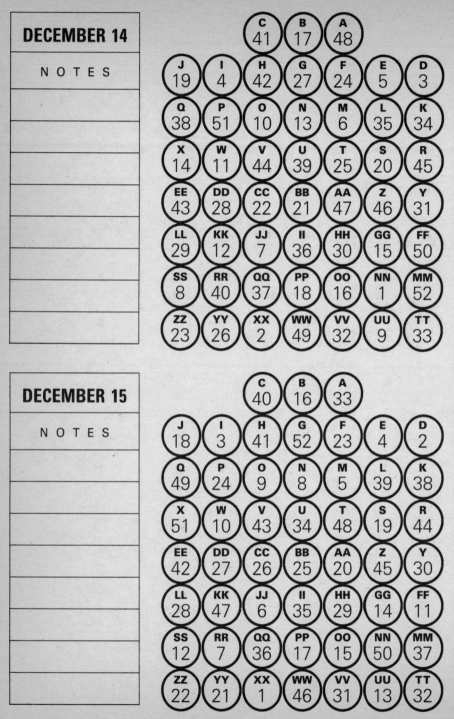

DECEMBER 14

NOTES

DECEMBER 15

NOTES

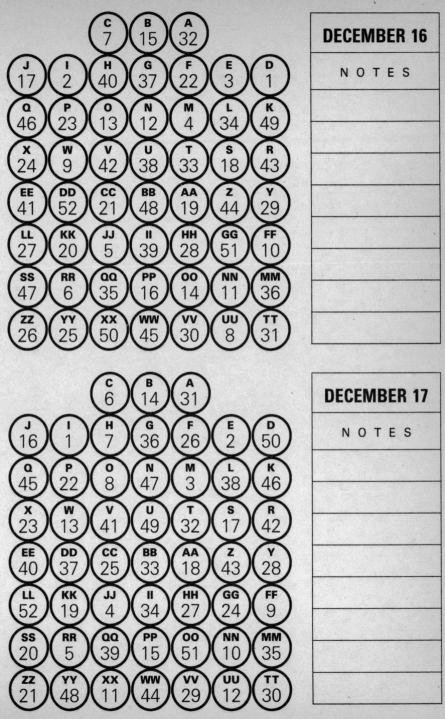

DECEMBER 16

NOTES

DECEMBER 17

NOTES

DECEMBER 18

NOTES

		C 38	B 13	A 51	
J 10	I 43	H 34	G 48	F 19	E 44	D 42
Q 27	P 20	O 5	N 3	M 45	L 30	K 28
X 47	W 6	V 35	U 29	T 14	S 11	R 36
EE 39	DD 25	CC 17	BB 15	AA 50	Z 37	Y 22
LL 21	KK 1	JJ 46	II 31	HH 26	GG 12	FF 7
SS 2	RR 49	QQ 32	PP 9	OO 8	NN 40	MM 33
ZZ 18	YY 16	XX 41	WW 52	VV 23	UU 4	TT 24

DECEMBER 19

NOTES

		C 46	B 12	A 23	
J 13	I 41	H 49	G 32	F 17	E 42	D 40
Q 37	P 18	O 3	N 1	M 43	L 28	K 52
X 19	W 4	V 34	U 27	T 24	S 9	R 39
EE 38	DD 33	CC 15	BB 51	AA 10	Z 35	Y 21
LL 48	KK 11	JJ 44	II 29	HH 25	GG 20	FF 5
SS 50	RR 45	QQ 30	PP 8	OO 47	NN 6	MM 31
ZZ 16	YY 14	XX 7	WW 36	VV 26	UU 2	TT 22

190

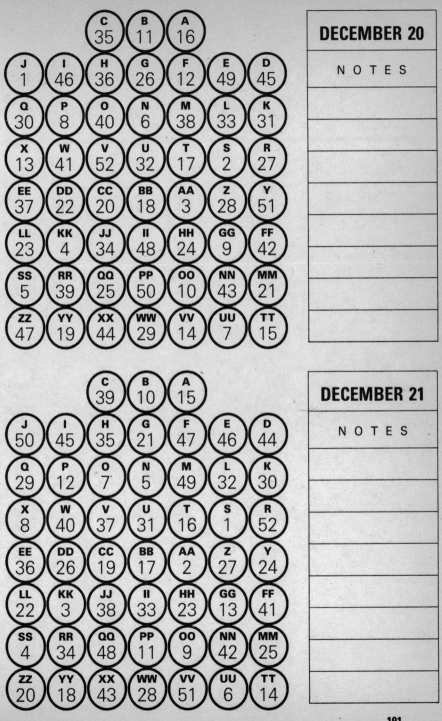

DECEMBER 20

NOTES

DECEMBER 21

NOTES

191

DECEMBER 22

NOTES

| C 34 | B 9 | A 14 |

| J 11 | I 44 | H 39 | G 25 | F 20 | E 45 | D 43 |

| Q 28 | P 47 | O 6 | N 4 | M 46 | L 31 | K 29 |

| X 12 | W 7 | V 36 | U 30 | T 15 | S 50 | R 37 |

| EE 35 | DD 21 | CC 18 | BB 16 | AA 1 | Z 52 | Y 23 |

| LL 26 | KK 2 | JJ 49 | II 32 | HH 22 | GG 8 | FF 40 |

| SS 3 | RR 38 | QQ 33 | PP 10 | OO 13 | NN 41 | MM 48 |

| ZZ 19 | YY 17 | XX 42 | WW 27 | VV 24 | UU 5 | TT 51 |

DECEMBER 23

NOTES

| C 49 | B 8 | A 24 |

| J 9 | I 42 | H 38 | G 33 | F 18 | E 43 | D 41 |

| Q 52 | P 19 | O 4 | N 2 | M 44 | L 29 | K 27 |

| X 20 | W 5 | V 39 | U 28 | T 51 | S 10 | R 35 |

| EE 34 | DD 48 | CC 16 | BB 14 | AA 11 | Z 36 | Y 26 |

| LL 25 | KK 50 | JJ 45 | II 30 | HH 21 | GG 47 | FF 6 |

| SS 1 | RR 46 | QQ 31 | PP 13 | OO 12 | NN 7 | MM 32 |

| ZZ 17 | YY 15 | XX 40 | WW 37 | VV 22 | UU 3 | TT 23 |

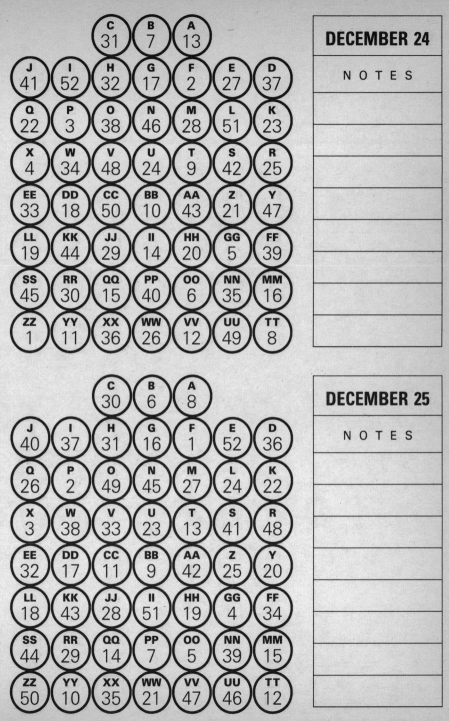

DECEMBER 24

NOTES

C	B	A
31	7	13

J	I	H	G	F	E	D
41	52	32	17	2	27	37

Q	P	O	N	M	L	K
22	3	38	46	28	51	23

X	W	V	U	T	S	R
4	34	48	24	9	42	25

EE	DD	CC	BB	AA	Z	Y
33	18	50	10	43	21	47

LL	KK	JJ	II	HH	GG	FF
19	44	29	14	20	5	39

SS	RR	QQ	PP	OO	NN	MM
45	30	15	40	6	35	16

ZZ	YY	XX	WW	VV	UU	TT
1	11	36	26	12	49	8

DECEMBER 25

NOTES

C	B	A
30	6	8

J	I	H	G	F	E	D
40	37	31	16	1	52	36

Q	P	O	N	M	L	K
26	2	49	45	27	24	22

X	W	V	U	T	S	R
3	38	33	23	13	41	48

EE	DD	CC	BB	AA	Z	Y
32	17	11	9	42	25	20

LL	KK	JJ	II	HH	GG	FF
18	43	28	51	19	4	34

SS	RR	QQ	PP	OO	NN	MM
44	29	14	7	5	39	15

ZZ	YY	XX	WW	VV	UU	TT
50	10	35	21	47	46	12

DECEMBER 26

NOTES

			C 29	B 5	A 12	
J 7	I 36	H 30	G 15	F 50	E 37	D 35
Q 21	P 1	O 46	N 44	M 52	L 23	K 26
X 2	W 49	V 32	U 22	T 8	S 40	R 33
EE 31	DD 16	CC 10	BB 13	AA 41	Z 48	Y 19
LL 17	KK 42	JJ 27	II 24	HH 18	GG 3	FF 38
SS 43	RR 28	QQ 51	PP 6	OO 4	NN 34	MM 14
ZZ 11	YY 9	XX 39	WW 25	VV 20	UU 45	TT 47

DECEMBER 27

NOTES

			C 28	B 4	A 47	
J 6	I 35	H 29	G 14	F 11	E 36	D 39
Q 25	P 50	O 45	N 43	M 37	L 22	K 21
X 1	W 46	V 31	U 26	T 12	S 7	R 32
EE 30	DD 15	CC 9	BB 8	AA 40	Z 33	Y 18
LL 16	KK 41	JJ 52	II 23	HH 17	GG 2	FF 49
SS 42	RR 27	QQ 24	PP 5	OO 3	NN 38	MM 51
ZZ 10	YY 13	XX 34	WW 48	VV 19	UU 44	TT 20

DECEMBER 28

NOTES

DECEMBER 29

NOTES

195

DECEMBER 30

NOTES

		C 37	B 1	A 18		
J 3	I 38	H 52	G 23	F 13	E 34	D 49
Q 32	P 9	O 42	N 40	M 39	L 25	K 33
X 10	W 43	V 28	U 48	T 19	S 4	R 29
EE 27	DD 24	CC 12	BB 20	AA 5	Z 30	Y 15
LL 51	KK 6	JJ 35	II 21	HH 14	GG 11	FF 44
SS 7	RR 36	QQ 26	PP 2	OO 50	NN 45	MM 22
ZZ 8	YY 47	XX 46	WW 31	VV 16	UU 41	TT 17

DECEMBER 31

NOTES

		C 18	B 52	A 43		
J 28	I 51	H 19	G 4	F 34	E 14	D 24
Q 9	P 39	O 25	N 33	M 15	L 50	K 10
X 35	W 21	V 47	U 11	T 44	S 29	R 12
EE 20	DD 5	CC 49	BB 45	AA 30	Z 8	Y 40
LL 6	KK 31	JJ 16	II 1	HH 7	GG 36	FF 26
SS 32	RR 17	QQ 2	PP 27	OO 37	NN 22	MM 3
ZZ 38	YY 46	XX 23	WW 13	VV 41	UU 48	TT 42

PICK LISTS
1 through 10

PICK LIST 1

BALL	1st GROUP	2nd GROUP	3rd GROUP
A	E	AA	EE
B	F	BB	B
C	G	CC	Y
D	H	Y	JJ
E	I	Z	KK
F	J	HH	LL
G	K	II	M
H	L	JJ	FF
I	M	DD	GG
J	N	EE	HH
K	O	FF	QQ
L	P	GG	RR
M	Q	OO	SS
N	R	PP	T
O	S	QQ	MM
P	T	KK	NN
Q	U	LL	OO
R	V	MM	XX
S	W	NN	YY
T	X	VV	ZZ
U	Y	WW	KK
V	Z	XX	TT
W	AA	RR	UU
X	BB	SS	VV
Y	CC	TT	C
Z	DD	UU	HH

BALL	1st GROUP	2nd GROUP	3rd GROUP
AA	EE	A	QQ
BB	FF	B	ZZ
CC	GG	C	SS
DD	HH	YY	LL
EE	II	ZZ	A
FF	JJ	D	H
GG	KK	E	I
HH	LL	F	J
II	MM	G	YY
JJ	NN	H	D
KK	OO	I	E
LL	PP	J	F
MM	QQ	K	O
NN	RR	L	P
OO	SS	M	Q
PP	TT	N	XX
QQ	UU	O	K
RR	VV	P	L
SS	WW	Q	M
TT	XX	R	V
UU	YY	S	W
VV	ZZ	T	X
WW	A	U	WW
XX	B	V	R
YY	C	W	S
ZZ	D	X	T

PICK LIST 2

BALL	1st GROUP	2nd GROUP	3rd GROUP
A	B C	VV OO	G O
B	C D	WW PP	H P
C	D E	XX QQ	I Q
D	E F	TT MM	L T
E	F G	UU NN	M U
F	G H	A VV	L R
G	H I	B WW	O W
H	I J	C XX	P X
I	J K	YY RR	O U
J	K L	ZZ SS	P V
K	L M	D TT	E A
L	M N	E UU	F B
M	N O	F A	S Y
N	O P	G B	T Z
O	P Q	H C	U AA
P	Q R	I YY	V BB
Q	R S	J ZZ	W CC
R	S T	K D	Z HH
S	T U	L E	M G
T	U V	M F	Z FF
U	V W	N G	O I
V	W X	O H	DD LL
W	X Y	P I	O G
X	Y Z	Q J	DD JJ
Y	Z AA	R K	GG OO
Z	AA BB	S L	T N

BALL	1st GROUP	2nd GROUP	3rd GROUP
AA	BB CC	T M	GG MM
BB	CC DD	U N	JJ RR
CC	DD EE	V O	KK SS
DD	EE FF	W P	V N
EE	FF GG	X Q	KK QQ
FF	GG HH	Y R	NN VV
GG	HH II	Z S	AA U
HH	II JJ	AA T	NN TT
II	JJ KK	BB U	QQ YY
JJ	KK LL	CC V	RR ZZ
KK	LL MM	DD W	QQ WW
LL	MM NN	EE X	RR XX
MM	NN OO	FF Y	GG AA
NN	OO PP	GG Z	HH BB
OO	PP QQ	HH AA	II CC
PP	QQ RR	II BB	JJ DD
QQ	RR SS	JJ CC	KK EE
RR	SS TT	KK DD	JJ BB
SS	TT UU	LL EE	KK CC
TT	UU VV	MM FF	NN HH
UU	VV WW	NN GG	OO II
VV	WW XX	OO HH	NN FF
WW	XX YY	PP II	QQ KK
XX	YY ZZ	QQ JJ	RR LL
YY	ZZ A	RR KK	QQ II
ZZ	A B	SS LL	RR JJ

PICK LIST 3

BALL	1st GROUP	2nd GROUP	3rd GROUP
A	B C D	VV OO HH	G O W
B	C D E	WW PP II	H P X
C	D E F	XX QQ JJ	G M S
D	E F G	TT MM FF	L T BB
E	F G H	UU NN GG	M U CC
F	G H I	A VV OO	N V DD
G	H I J	B WW PP	O W EE
H	I J K	C XX QQ	B P X
I	J K L	YY RR KK	O U AA
J	K L M	ZZ SS LL	P V BB
K	L M N	D TT MM	S AA II
L	M N O	E UU NN	F B R
M	N O P	F A VV	U CC KK
N	O P Q	G B WW	V DD LL
O	P Q R	H C XX	U AA GG
P	Q R S	I YY RR	V BB HH
Q	R S T	J ZZ SS	W CC II
R	S T U	K D TT	L F B
S	T U V	L E UU	M G C
T	U V W	M F A	N H Z
U	V W X	N G B	CC KK SS
V	W X Y	O H C	P J BB
W	X Y Z	P I YY	O G A
X	Y Z AA	Q J ZZ	P H B
Y	Z AA BB	R K D	GG OO WW
Z	AA BB CC	S L E	HH PP XX

BALL	1st GROUP	2nd GROUP	3rd GROUP
AA	BB CC DD	T M F	II QQ YY
BB	CC DD EE	U N G	JJ RR ZZ
CC	DD EE FF	V O H	U M E
DD	EE FF GG	W P I	V N F
EE	FF GG HH	X Q J	KK QQ WW
FF	GG HH II	Y R K	Z T N
GG	HH II JJ	Z S L	Y OO WW
HH	II JJ KK	AA T M	Z PP XX
II	JJ KK LL	BB U N	AA S K
JJ	KK LL MM	CC V O	DD X PP
KK	LL MM NN	DD W P	EE QQ WW
LL	MM NN OO	EE X Q	DD V N
MM	NN OO PP	FF Y R	GG AA U
NN	OO PP QQ	GG Z S	TT HH BB
OO	PP QQ RR	HH AA T	WW GG Y
PP	QQ RR SS	II BB U	HH Z R
QQ	RR SS TT	JJ CC V	WW KK EE
RR	SS TT UU	KK DD W	ZZ JJ BB
SS	TT UU VV	LL EE X	KK CC U
TT	UU VV WW	MM FF Y	NN HH BB
UU	VV WW XX	NN GG Z	OO II CC
VV	WW XX YY	OO HH AA	PP JJ DD
WW	XX YY ZZ	PP II BB	OO GG Y
XX	YY ZZ A	QQ JJ CC	PP HH Z
YY	ZZ A B	RR KK DD	QQ II AA
ZZ	A B C	SS LL EE	RR JJ BB

PICK LIST 4

BALL	1st GROUP	2nd GROUP	3rd GROUP
A	B C D E	VV OO HH AA	G O W EE
B	C D E F	WW PP II BB	H P X F
C	D E F G	XX QQ JJ CC	G M S Y
D	E F G H	TT MM FF Y	L T BB JJ
E	F G H I	UU NN GG Z	M U CC KK
F	G H I J	A VV OO HH	N V DD LL
G	H I J K	B WW PP II	C M S Y
H	I J K L	C XX QQ JJ	N T Z FF
I	J K L M	YY RR KK DD	O U AA GG
J	K L M N	ZZ SS LL EE	P V BB HH
K	L M N O	D TT MM FF	S AA II QQ
L	M N O P	E UU NN GG	T BB JJ RR
M	N O P Q	F A VV OO	U CC KK SS
N	O P Q R	G B WW PP	H T Z FF
O	P Q R S	H C XX QQ	U AA GG MM
P	Q R S T	I YY RR KK	V BB HH NN
Q	R S T U	J ZZ SS LL	W CC II OO
R	S T U V	K D TT MM	Z HH PP XX
S	T U V W	L E UU NN	AA II QQ YY
T	U V W X	M F A VV	BB JJ RR ZZ
U	V W X Y	N G B WW	M CC KK SS
V	W X Y Z	O H C XX	BB HH NN TT
W	X Y Z AA	P I YY RR	CC II OO UU
X	Y Z AA BB	Q J ZZ SS	DD JJ PP VV
Y	Z AA BB CC	R K D TT	S M G C
Z	AA BB CC DD	S L E UU	FF T N H

PICK LIST 4 (continued)

BALL	1st GROUP	2nd GROUP	3rd GROUP
AA	BB CC DD EE	T M F A	S II QQ YY
BB	CC DD EE FF	U N G B	JJ T L D
CC	DD EE FF GG	V O H C	W II OO UU
DD	EE FF GG HH	W P I YY	X JJ PP VV
EE	FF GG HH II	X Q J ZZ	W O G A
FF	GG HH II JJ	Y R K D	Z T N H
GG	HH II JJ KK	Z S L E	AA U O I
HH	II JJ KK LL	AA T M F	BB V P J
II	JJ KK LL MM	BB U N G	QQ AA S K
JJ	KK LL MM NN	CC V O H	BB T L D
KK	LL MM NN OO	DD W P I	CC U M E
LL	MM NN OO PP	EE X Q J	DD V N F
MM	NN OO PP QQ	FF Y R K	GG AA U O
NN	OO PP QQ RR	GG Z S L	HH BB V P
OO	PP QQ RR SS	HH AA T M	II CC W Q
PP	QQ RR SS TT	II BB U N	VV JJ DD X
QQ	RR SS TT UU	JJ CC V O	II AA S K
RR	SS TT UU VV	KK DD W P	JJ BB T L
SS	TT UU VV WW	LL EE X Q	KK CC U M
TT	UU VV WW XX	MM FF Y R	NN HH BB V
UU	VV WW XX YY	NN GG Z S	OO II CC W
VV	WW XX YY ZZ	OO HH AA T	PP JJ DD X
WW	XX YY ZZ A	PP II BB U	VV JJ DD X
XX	YY ZZ A B	QQ JJ CC V	PP HH Z R
YY	ZZ A B C	RR KK DD W	QQ II AA S
ZZ	A B C D	SS LL EE X	RR JJ BB T

PICK LIST 5

BALL	1st GROUP	2nd GROUP	3rd GROUP
A	B C D E F	VV OO HH AA T	EE W O G E
B	C D E F G	WW PP II BB U	X P H F L
C	D E F G H	XX QQ JJ CC V	I G M S Y
D	E F G H I	TT MM FF Y R	L T BB JJ RR
E	F G H I J	UU NN GG Z S	M U CC KK SS
F	G H I J K	A VV OO HH AA	N V DD LL L
G	H I J K L	B WW PP II BB	O W EE A C
H	I J K L M	C XX QQ JJ CC	P X B N T
I	J K L M N	YY RR KK DD W	O U AA GG MM
J	K L M N O	ZZ SS LL EE X	P V BB HH NN
K	L M N O P	D TT MM FF Y	S AA II QQ YY
L	M N O P Q	E UU NN GG Z	T BB JJ RR ZZ
M	N O P Q R	F A VV OO HH	SS KK CC U E
N	O P Q R S	G B WW PP II	LL DD V N F
O	P Q R S T	H C XX QQ JJ	I U AA GG MM
P	Q R S T U	I YY RR KK DD	V BB HH NN TT
Q	R S T U V	J ZZ SS LL EE	W CC II OO UU
R	S T U V W	K D TT MM FF	R Z HH PP XX
S	T U V W X	L E UU NN GG	AA II QQ YY K
T	U V W X Y	M F A VV OO	BB JJ RR ZZ L
U	V W X Y Z	N G B WW PP	SS KK CC M E
V	W X Y Z AA	O H C XX QQ	P BB HH NN TT
W	X Y Z AA BB	P I YY RR KK	Q CC II OO UU
X	Y Z AA BB CC	Q J ZZ SS LL	DD JJ PP VV X
Y	Z AA BB CC DD	R K D TT MM	S M GG OO WW
Z	AA BB CC DD EE	S L E UU NN	H N T Z FF

PICK LIST 5 (continued)

BALL	1st GROUP	2nd GROUP	3rd GROUP
AA	BB CC DD EE FF	T M F A V V	U O I GG MM
BB	CC DD EE FF GG	U N G B WW	JJ RR ZZ T L
CC	DD EE FF GG HH	V O H C XX	KK SS U M E
DD	EE FF GG HH II	W P I YY RR	X DD JJ PP VV
EE	FF GG HH II JJ	X Q J ZZ SS	KK W O G A
FF	GG HH II JJ KK	Y R K D TT	Z T N H NN
GG	HH II JJ KK LL	Z S L E UU	MM AA U O I
HH	II JJ KK LL MM	AA T M F A	NN BB V P J
II	JJ KK LL MM NN	BB U N G B	QQ YY AA S K
JJ	KK LL MM NN OO	CC V O H C	ZZ RR BB T L
KK	LL MM NN OO PP	DD W P I YY	SS CC U M E
LL	MM NN OO PP QQ	EE X Q J ZZ	RR DD V N F
MM	NN OO PP QQ RR	FF Y R K D	GG AA U O I
NN	OO PP QQ RR SS	GG Z S L E	HH BB V P J
OO	PP QQ RR SS TT	HH AA T M F	UU II CC W Q
PP	QQ RR SS TT UU	II BB U N G	X DD JJ PP VV
QQ	RR SS TT UU VV	JJ CC V O H	YY II AA S K
RR	SS TT UU VV WW	KK DD W P I	ZZ JJ BB T L
SS	TT UU VV WW XX	LL EE X Q J	KK CC U M E
TT	UU VV WW XX YY	MM FF Y R K	NN HH BB V P
UU	VV WW XX YY ZZ	NN GG Z S L	OO II CC W Q
VV	WW XX YY ZZ A	OO HH AA T M	PP JJ DD X NN
WW	XX YY ZZ A B	PP II BB U N	QQ KK EE OO GG
XX	YY ZZ A B C	QQ JJ CC V O	XX PP HH Z R
YY	ZZ A B C D	RR KK DD W P	QQ II AA S K
ZZ	A B C D E	SS LL EE X Q	RR JJ BB T L

PICK LIST 6

BALL	1st GROUP	2nd GROUP	3rd GROUP
A	B C D E F G	VV OO HH AA T M	EE W O G A E
B	C D E F G H	WW PP II BB U N	H P X F L R
C	D E F G H I	XX QQ JJ CC V O	Q I G M S Y
D	E F G H I J	TT MM FF Y R K	L T BB JJ RR ZZ
E	F G H I J K	UU NN GG Z S L	SS KK CC U M E
F	G H I J K L	A VV OO HH AA T	LL DD V N L R
G	H I J K L M	B WW PP II BB U	EE W O G A C
H	I J K L M N	C XX QQ JJ CC V	X P N T Z FF
I	J K L M N O	YY RR KK DD W P	Q O U AA GG MM
J	K L M N O P	ZZ SS LL EE X Q	P V BB HH NN TT
K	L M N O P Q	D TT MM FF Y R	YY QQ II AA S K
L	M N O P Q R	E UU NN GG Z S	ZZ RR JJ BB T D
M	N O P Q R S	F A VV OO HH AA	SS KK CC U M E
N	O P Q R S T	G B WW PP II BB	V DD LL F H T
O	P Q R S T U	H C XX QQ JJ CC	EE W O G A I
P	Q R S T U V	I YY RR KK DD W	J V BB HH NN TT
Q	R S T U V W	J ZZ SS LL EE X	W CC II OO UU I
R	S T U V W X	K D TT MM FF Y	XX PP HH Z L F
S	T U V W X Y	L E UU NN GG Z	YY QQ II AA S K
T	U V W X Y Z	M F A VV OO HH	ZZ RR JJ BB L D
U	V W X Y Z AA	N G B WW PP II	SS KK CC U M E
V	W X Y Z AA BB	O H C XX QQ JJ	J P BB HH NN TT
W	X Y Z AA BB CC	P I YY RR KK DD	Q W CC II OO UU
X	Y Z AA BB CC DD	Q J ZZ SS LL EE	H P DD JJ PP VV
Y	Z AA BB CC DD EE	R K D TT MM FF	WW OO GG S M G
Z	AA BB CC DD EE FF	S L E UU NN GG	HH PP XX T N H

BALL	1st GROUP	2nd GROUP	3rd GROUP
AA	BB CC DD EE FF GG	T M F A VV OO	YY QQ II AA S K
BB	CC DD EE FF GG HH	U N G B WW PP	ZZ RR JJ T L D
CC	DD EE FF GG HH II	V O H C XX QQ	Q W CC II OO UU
DD	EE FF GG HH II JJ	W P I YY RR KK	X DD JJ PP VV LL
EE	FF GG HH II JJ KK	X Q J ZZ SS LL	KK QQ WW W O G
FF	GG HH II JJ KK LL	Y R K D TT MM	H N T Z NN VV
GG	HH II JJ KK LL MM	Z S L E UU NN	I O U AA GG MM
HH	II JJ KK LL MM NN	AA T M F A VV	J P V BB NN TT
II	JJ KK LL MM NN OO	BB U N G B WW	YY QQ II AA S K
JJ	KK LL MM NN OO PP	CC V O H C XX	ZZ RR BB T L D
KK	LL MM NN OO PP QQ	DD W P I YY RR	SS EE KK QQ WW CC
LL	MM NN OO PP QQ RR	EE X Q J ZZ SS	DD V N F RR XX
MM	NN OO PP QQ RR SS	FF Y R K D TT	I O U AA GG UU
NN	OO PP QQ RR SS TT	GG Z S L E UU	J P V BB HH TT
OO	PP QQ RR SS TT UU	HH AA T M F A	Q W CC II OO UU
PP	QQ RR SS TT UU VV	II BB U N G B	X DD JJ VV XX HH
QQ	RR SS TT UU VV WW	JJ CC V O H C	YY QQ II AA S K
RR	SS TT UU VV WW XX	KK DD W P I YY	ZZ JJ BB T L D
SS	TT UU VV WW XX YY	LL EE X Q J ZZ	SS KK CC U M E
TT	UU VV WW XX YY ZZ	MM FF Y R K D	J P V BB HH NN
UU	VV WW XX YY ZZ A	NN GG Z S L E	Q W CC II OO UU
VV	WW XX YY ZZ A B	OO HH AA T M F	X DD JJ PP NN FF
WW	XX YY ZZ A B C	PP II BB U N G	EE KK QQ OO GG Y
XX	YY ZZ A B C D	QQ JJ CC V O H	LL RR PP HH Z R
YY	ZZ A B C D E	RR KK DD W P I	SS QQ II AA S K
ZZ	A B C D E F	SS LL EE X Q J	RR JJ BB T L D

PICK LIST 7

BALL	1st GROUP	2nd GROUP	3rd GROUP
A	B C D E F G H	VV OO HH AA T M F	EE W O G A E K
B	C D E F G H I	WW PP II BB U N G	X P H B F L R
C	D E F G H I J	XX QQ JJ CC V O H	Q I C G M S Y
D	E F G H I J K	TT MM FF Y R K D	ZZ RR JJ BB T L D
E	F G H I J K L	UU NN GG Z S L E	SS KK CC U M E K
F	G H I J K L M	A VV OO HH AA T M	LL DD VN B L R
G	H I J K L M N	B WW PP II BB U N	EE W O A C M S
H	I J K L M N O	C XX QQ JJ CC V O	X P B N T Z FF
I	J K L M N O	YY RR KK DD W P I	Q C O U AA GG MM
J	K L M N O P Q	ZZ SS LL EE X Q J	J P V BB HH NN TT
K	L M N O P Q R	D TT MM FF Y R K	A E S AA II QQ YY
L	M N O P Q R S	E UU NN GG Z S L	ZZ RR JJ BB T L D
M	N O P Q R S T	F A VV OO HH AA T	G S E U CC KK SS
N	O P Q R S T U	G B WW PP II BB U	H T Z LL DD V F
O	P Q R S T U V	H C XX QQ JJ CC V	EE W G A I U AA
P	Q R S T U V W	I YY RR KK DD W P	J V BB HH NN TT X
Q	R S T U V W X	J ZZ SS LL EE X Q	I C W CC II OO UU
R	S T U V W X Y	K D TT MM FF Y R	L F B Z HH PP XX
S	T U V W X Y Z	L E UU NN GG Z S	M Y K AA II QQ YY
T	U V W X Y Z AA	M F A VV OO HH AA	ZZ RR JJ BB T L D
U	V W X Y Z AA BB	N G B WW PP II BB	O AA SS KK CC M E
V	W X Y Z AA BB CC	O H C XX QQ JJ CC	LL DD N F J P BB
W	X Y Z AA BB CC DD	P I YY RR KK DD W	Q CC II OO UU EE O
X	Y Z AA BB CC DD EE	Q J ZZ SS LL EE X	P H B DD JJ PP VV
Y	Z AA BB CC DD EE FF	R K D TT MM FF Y	S M G C GG OO WW
Z	AA BB CC DD EE FF GG	S L E UU NN GG Z	XX PP HH R N T FF

BALL	1st GROUP	2nd GROUP	3rd GROUP
AA	BB CC DD EE FF GG HH	T M F A VV OO HH	YY QQ II S K U GG
BB	CC DD EE FF GG HH II	U N G B WW PP II	ZZ RR JJ BB T L D
CC	DD EE FF GG HH II JJ	V O H C XX QQ JJ	SS KK U M E W II
DD	EE FF GG HH II JJ KK	W P I YY RR KK DD	LL V N F X JJ PP
EE	FF GG HH II JJ KK LL	X Q J ZZ SS LL EE	W O G A KK QQ WW
FF	GG HH II JJ KK LL MM	Y R K D TT MM FF	VV NN FF H N T Z
GG	HH II JJ KK LL MM NN	Z S L E UU NN GG	I O U AA MM OO Y
HH	II JJ KK LL MM NN OO	AA T M F A VV OO	XX PP Z R BB NN TT
II	JJ KK LL MM NN OO PP	BB U N G B WW PP	CC OO YY QQ AA S K
JJ	KK LL MM NN OO PP QQ	CC V O H C XX QQ	ZZ RR JJ BB T L D
KK	LL MM NN OO PP QQ RR	DD W P I YY RR KK	SS CC U M E E QQ
LL	MM NN OO PP QQ RR SS	EE X Q J ZZ SS LL	LL DD V N F RR XX
MM	NN OO PP QQ RR SS TT	FF Y R K D TT MM	UU MM GG AA U O I
NN	OO PP QQ RR SS TT UU	GG Z S L E UU NN	VV FF TT HH BB V P
OO	PP QQ RR SS TT UU VV	HH AA T M F A VV	WW GG Y UU II CC W
PP	QQ RR SS TT UU VV WW	II BB U N G B WW	XX HH Z VV JJ DD X
QQ	RR SS TT UU VV WW XX	JJ CC V O H C XX	YY II AA S K WW KK
RR	SS TT UU VV WW XX YY	KK DD W P I YY RR	LL XX ZZ JJ BB T L
SS	TT UU VV WW XX YY ZZ	LL EE X Q J ZZ SS	SS YY KK CC U M E
TT	UU VV WW XX YY ZZ A	MM FF Y R K D TT	TT NN HH BB V P J
UU	VV WW XX YY ZZ A B	NN GG Z S L E UU	MM UU OO II CC W Q
VV	WW XX YY ZZ A B C	OO HH AA T M F A	VV NN FF PP JJ DD X
WW	XX YY ZZ A B C D	PP II BB U N G B	WW OO GG Y QQ KK EE
XX	YY ZZ A B C D E	QQ JJ CC V O H C	XX RR LL PP HH Z R
YY	ZZ A B C D E F	RR KK DD W P I YY	YY SS QQ II AA S K
ZZ	A B C D E F G	SS LL EE X Q J ZZ	ZZ RR JJ BB T L D

PICK LIST 8

BALL	1st GROUP	2nd GROUP	3rd GROUP
A	B C D E F G H I	VV OO HH AA T M F A	E K G O WEE B H
B	C D E F G H I J	WW PP II BB U N G B	F L R H P X C A
C	D E F G H I J K	XX QQ JJ CC V O H C	B C I Q G M S Y
D	E F G H I J K L	TT MM FF Y R K D U U	K D L T BB JJ RR ZZ
E	F G H I J K L M	UU NN GG Z S L VV OO	SS KK CC U M E A K
F	G H I J K L M N	A VV OO HH AA T M WW	LL DD V N F B L R
G	H I J K L M N O	B WW PP II BB U N G	EE W O A C M S Y
H	I J K L M N O P	C XX QQ JJ CC V O H	X P H B N T Z F F
I	J K L M N O P Q	YY RR KK DD W P I ZZ	QI C O U AA GG MM
J	K L M N O P Q R	ZZ SS LL EE X Q J YY	I J P V BB HH NN TT
K	L M N O P Q R S	D TT MM FF Y R K UU	YY QQ II AA S K E A
L	M N O P Q R S T	E UU NN GG Z S L VV	ZZ RR JJ BB T D F R
M	N O P Q R S T U	F A VV OO HH AA T M	SS KK CC U E G S Y
N	O P Q R S T U V	G B WW PP II BB U N	LL DD V F H T Z FF
O	P Q R S T U V W	H C XX QQ JJ CC V O	EE W G A I U AA GG
P	Q R S T U V W X	I YY RR KK DD W P ZZ	X H B J V BB HH NN
Q	R S T U V W X Y	J ZZ SS LL EE X Q YY	QI C W CC II OO UU
R	S T U V W X Y Z	K D TT MM FF Y UU NN	XX PP HH Z R L F B
S	T U V W X Y Z AA	L E UU NN GG Z S TT	YY QQ II AA K G M Y
T	U V W X Y Z AA BB	M F A VV OO HH A T	ZZ RR JJ BB L D N Z
U	V W X Y Z AA BB CC	N G B WW PP II BB U	SS KK CC U M E O AA
V	W X Y Z AA BB CC DD	O H C XX QQ JJ CC V	J P V BB HH NN TT N
W	X Y Z AA BB CC DD EE	P I YY RR KK DD W ZZ	EE W O G A Q CC II
X	Y Z AA BB CC DD EE FF	Q J ZZ SS LL EE X YY	X P H B DD JJ PP VV
Y	Z AA BB CC DD EE FF GG	R K D TT MM FF Y UU	Y S M G C GG OO WW
Z	AA BB CC DD EE FF GG HH	S L E UU NN GG Z TT	XX PP HH Z R N T FF

BALL	1st GROUP	2nd GROUP	3rd GROUP
AA	BB CC DD EE FF GG HH II	T M F A VV OO HH AA	YY QQ II AA S K U GG
BB	CC DD EE FF GG HH II JJ	U N G B WW PP II BB	ZZ RR JJ BB T L V HH
CC	DD EE FF GG HH II JJ KK	V O H C XX QQ JJ CC	SS KK U M Q W II OO
DD	EE FF GG HH II JJ KK LL	W P I YY RR KK DD ZZ	LL DD V N F X JJ PP
EE	FF GG HH II JJ KK LL MM	X Q J ZZ SS LL EE YY	EE W O G A KK QQ WW
FF	GG HH II JJ KK LL MM NN	Y R K D TT MM FF UU	H N T Z FF NN VV Y
GG	HH II JJ KK LL MM NN OO	Z S L E UU NN GG TT	WW OO GG Y O U AA MM
HH	II JJ KK LL MM NN OO PP	AA T M F A VV OO HH	XX PP HH Z R V BB NN
II	JJ KK LL MM NN OO PP QQ	BB U N G B WW PP II	YY QQ II AA S CC OO UU
JJ	KK LL MM NN OO PP QQ RR	CC V O H C XX QQ JJ	ZZ RR JJ BB T DD PP VV
KK	LL MM NN OO PP QQ RR SS	DD W P I YY RR KK ZZ	SS KK CC U M EE QQ WW
LL	MM NN OO PP QQ RR SS TT	EE X Q J ZZ SS LL YY	F N V DD LL KK RR XX
MM	NN OO PP QQ RR SS TT UU	FF Y R K D TT MM UU	UU MM TT GG AA U O I
NN	OO PP QQ RR SS TT UU VV	GG Z S L E UU NN TT	P V BB HH NN TT VV FF
OO	PP QQ RR SS TT UU VV WW	HH AA T M F A VV OO	WW OO GG Y W CC II UU
PP	QQ RR SS TT UU VV WW XX	II BB U N G B WW PP	XX PP HH Z X DD JJ VV
QQ	RR SS TT UU VV WW XX YY	JJ CC V O H C XX QQ	YY QQ II AA S EE KK WW
RR	SS TT UU VV WW XX YY ZZ	KK DD W P I YY RR ZZ	ZZ RR JJ BB T L LL XX
SS	TT UU VV WW XX YY ZZ A	LL EE X Q J ZZ SS YY	YY SS RR KK CC U M E
TT	UU VV WW XX YY ZZ A B	MM FF Y R K D TT UU	J P V BB HH NN TT MM
UU	VV WW XX YY ZZ A B C	NN GG Z S L E UU TT	Q W CC II OO UU TT MM
VV	WW XX YY ZZ A B C D	OO HH AA T M F A VV	X DD JJ PP VV UU NN FF
WW	XX YY ZZ A B C D E	PP II BB U N G B WW	EE KK QQ WW VV OO GG Y
XX	YY ZZ A B C D E F	QQ JJ CC V O H C XX	LL RR XX WW PP HH Z R
YY	ZZ A B C D E F G	RR KK DD W P I YY XX	SS YY ZZ QQ II AA S K
ZZ	A B C D E F G H	SS LL EE X Q J ZZ YY	ZZ RR JJ BB T L D SS

BALL	1st GROUP	2nd GROUP	3rd GROUP
A	B C D E F G H I J	VV OO HH AA T M F A WW	EE W O G A B E K C
B	C D E F G H I J K	WW PP II BB U N G B XX	X P H B C F L R A
C	D E F G H I J K L	XX QQ JJ CC V O H C YY	Q I C G M S Y H B
D	E F G H I J K L M	TT MM FF Y R K D UU NN	ZZ RR JJ BB T L D E K
E	F G H I J K L M N	UU NN GG Z S L E TT MM	SS KK CC U M E A K D
F	G H I J K L M N O	A VV OO HH AA T M F UU	LL DD V N F B L R A
G	H I J K L M N O P	B WW PP II BB U N G VV	EE W O G A C M S Y
H	I J K L M N O P Q	C XX QQ JJ CC V O H WW	X P H B G N T Z FF
I	J K L M N O P Q R	YY RR KK DD W P I ZZ SS	Q I C J O U AA GG MM
J	K L M N O P Q R S	ZZ SS LL EE X Q J YY RR	J P V BB HH NN TT Q I
K	L M N O P Q R S T	D TT MM FF Y R K UU NN	YY QQ II AA S K A E D
L	M N O P Q R S T U	E UU NN GG Z S L TT MM	ZZ RR JJ BB T L D F R
M	N O P Q R S T U V	F A VV OO HH AA T M UU	SS KK CC U M E C G S
N	O P Q R S T U V W	G B WW PP II BB U N VV	LL DD V N F H T Z FF
O	P Q R S T U V W X	H C XX QQ JJ CC V O YY	EE W O G A I U AA GG
P	Q R S T U V W X Y	I YY RR KK DD W P ZZ SS	X P H B J V BB HH NN
Q	R S T U V W X Y Z	J ZZ SS LL EE X Q Y Y RR	Q I C J W CC II OO UU
R	S T U V W X Y Z AA	K D TT MM FF Y R UU NN	XX PP HH ZR B F L Y
S	T U V W X Y Z AA BB	L E UU NN GG Z S TT MM	YY QQ II AA S K G M Y
T	U V W X Y Z AA BB.CC	M F A VV OO HH AA T UU	ZZ RR JJ BB T L D N Z
U	V W X Y Z AA BB CC DD	N G B WW PP II BB U VV	SS KK CC U M E O AA GG
V	W X Y Z AA BB CC DD EE	O H C X QQ JJ CC V WW	LL DD V N F J P BB HH
W	X Y Z AA BB CC DD EE FF	P I YY RR KK DD W XX QQ	EE W O G A Q CC II OO
X	Y Z AA BB CC DD EE FF GG	Q J ZZ SS LL EE X YY RR	X P H B DD JJ PP VV W
Y	Z AA BB CC DD EE FF GG HH	R K D TT MM FF Y UU NN	C G M S Y GG OO WW FF
Z	AA BB CC DD EE FF GG HH II	S L E UU NN GG Z TT MM	XX PP HH ZR H N T FF

PICK LIST 9 (continued)

BALL	1st GROUP	2nd GROUP	3rd GROUP
AA	BB CC DD EE FF GG HH II JJ	T M F A VV OO HH AA UU	YY QQ II AA S K U GG MM
BB	CC DD EE FF GG HH II JJ KK	U N G B WW PP II BB VV	ZZ RR JJ BB T L D V HH
CC	DD EE FF GG HH II JJ KK LL	V O H C XX QQ JJ CC WW	SS KK CC U M E Q W II
DD	EE FF GG HH II JJ KK LL MM	W P I YY RR KK DD XX QQ	LL DD V N F X JJ PP VV
EE	FF GG HH II JJ KK LL MM NN	X Q J ZZ SS LL EE YY RR	EE W O G A DD KK QQ WW
FF	GG HH II JJ KK LL MM NN OO	Y R K D TT MM FF UU NN	VV NN FF Y MM H N T Z
GG	HH II JJ KK LL MM NN OO PP	Z S L E UU NN GG TT MM	WW OO GG Y I O U AA MM
HH	II JJ KK LL MM NN OO PP QQ	AA T M F A VV OO HH UU	XX PP HH Z R V BB NN TT
II	JJ KK LL MM NN OO PP QQ RR	BB U N G B WW PP II VV	YY QQ II AA S K CC OO UU
JJ	KK LL MM NN OO PP QQ RR SS	CC V O H C XX QQ JJ WW	ZZ RR JJ BB T L D DD PP
KK	LL MM NN OO PP QQ RR SS TT	DD W P I YY RR KK XX QQ	SS KK CC U M E EE QQ WW
LL	MM NN OO PP QQ RR SS TT UU	EE X Q J ZZ SS LL YY RR	LL DD V N F RR XX EE KK
MM	NN OO PP QQ RR SS TT UU VV	FF Y R K D TT MM UU NN	UU MM FF TT I O U AA GG
NN	OO PP QQ RR SS TT UU VV WW	GG Z S L E UU NN TT MM	VV NN FF J P V BB HH TT
OO	PP QQ RR SS TT UU VV WW XX	HH AA T M F A VV OO UU	WW OO GG Y Q W CC II UU
PP	QQ RR SS TT UU VV WW XX YY	II BB U N G B WW PP VV	XX PP HH Z R X DD JJ VV
QQ	RR SS TT UU VV WW XX YY ZZ	JJ CC V O H C XX QQ WW	YY QQ II AA S K EE KK WW
RR	SS TT UU VV WW XX YY ZZ A	KK DD W P I YY RR XX QQ	ZZ RR JJ BB T L D LL XX
SS	TT UU VV WW XX YY ZZ A B	LL EE X Q J ZZ SS YY RR	SS KK CC U M E LL ZZ YY
TT	UU VV WW XX YY ZZ A B C	MM FF Y R K D UU NN GG	J P V BB HH NN TT MM UU
UU	VV WW XX YY ZZ A B C D	NN GG Z S L E UU TT MM	Q W CC II OO UU VV MM TT
VV	WW XX YY ZZ A B C D E	VV OO HH AA T M F A UU	X DD JJ PP VV NN FF OO UU
WW	XX YY ZZ A B C D E F	PP II BB U N G B WW VV	EE KK QQ WW OO GG Y PP VV
XX	YY ZZ A B C D E F G	QQ JJ CC V O H C XX WW	LL RR XX PP HH Z R QQ WW
YY	ZZ A B C D E F G H	RR KK DD W P I YY XX QQ	YY QQ II AA S K SS RR XX
ZZ	A B C D E F G H I	SS LL EE X Q J ZZ YY RR	ZZ RR JJ BB T L D SS YY

PICK LIST 10

BALL	1st GROUP	2nd GROUP	3rd GROUP
A	B C D E F G H I J K	VV OO HH AA T MF A UU NN	EE W O G A B F L E K
B	C D E F G H I J K L	WW PP II BB U NG B VV OO	X P H B C G A F L R
C	D E F G H I J K L M	XX QQ JJ CC V O H C WW PP	C G M S Y Q I P H B
D	E F G H I J K L M N	TT MM FF Y R K D UU NN GG	A E K ZZ RR JJ BB T L D
E	F G H I J K L M N O	UU NN GG Z S L E TT MM FF	SS KK CC U ME A K D L
F	G H I J K L M N O P	A VV OO HH AA T MF UU NN	LL DD V N F B L R A E
G	H I J K L M N O P Q	B WW PP II BB U NG VV OO	EE W O G A C M S Y B
H	I J K L M N O P Q R	C XX QQ JJ CC V O H WW PP	X P H B C O N T Z FF
I	J K L M N O P Q R S	YY RR KK DD W P I XX QQ JJ	Q I C J P O U AA GG MM
J	K L M N O P Q R S T	ZZ SS LL EE X Q J YY RR KK	J P V BB HH NN TT Q I C
K	L M N O P Q R S T U	D TT MM FF Y R K UU NN GG	YY QQ II AA S K A E D R
L	M N O P Q R S T U V	E UU NN GG Z S L TT MM FF	ZZ RR JJ BB T L D B F R
M	N O P Q R S T U V W	F A VV OO HH AA T M UU NN	SS KK CC U ME C G S Y
N	O P Q R S T U V W X	G B WW PP II BB U N VV OO	LL DD V N F H T Z FF M
O	P Q R S T U V W X Y	H C XX QQ JJ CC V O WW PP	EE W O G A I U AA GG MM
P	Q R S T U V W X Y Z	I YY RR KK DD W P XX QQ JJ	J P V BB HH NN TT X H B
Q	R S T U V W X Y Z AA	J ZZ SS LL EE X Q YY RR KK	Q W CC II OO UU J P I C
R	S T U V W X Y Z AA BB	K D TT MM FF Y R UU NN GG	XX PP HH Z R B F L K Y
S	T U V W X Y Z AA BB CC	L E UU NN GG Z S TT MM FF	YY QQ II AA S K C G M Y
T	U V W X Y Z AA BB CC DD	M F A VV OO HH AA T UU NN	ZZ RR JJ BB T L D N Z FF
U	V W X Y Z AA BB CC DD EE	N G B WW PP II BB U VV OO	SS KK CC U ME I O AA GG
V	W X Y Z AA BB CC DD EE FF	O H C XX QQ JJ CC V WW PP	LL DD V N F J P BB HH NN
W	X Y Z AA BB CC DD EE FF GG	P I YY RR KK DD W XX QQ JJ	EE W O G A Q CC II OO UU
X	Y Z AA BB CC DD EE FF GG HH	Q J ZZ SS LL EE X YY RR KK	X P H B DD JJ PP VV Q W
Y	Z AA BB CC DD EE FF GG HH II	R K D TT MM FF Y UU NN GG	WW OO GG Y C G M S R FF
Z	AA BB CC DD EE FF GG HH II JJ	S L E UU NN GG Z TT MM FF	XX PP HH Z R H N T FF Y

PICK LIST 10 (continued)

BALL	1st GROUP	2nd GROUP	3rd GROUP
AA	BB CC DD EE FF GG HH II JJ KK	T M F A VV OO HH AA UU NN	YY QQ II AA S K O U GG MM
BB	CC DD EE FF GG HH II JJ KK LL	U N G B WW PP II BB VV OO	ZZ RR JJ BB T L D V HH NN
CC	DD EE FF GG HH II JJ KK LL MM	V O H C XX QQ JJ CC WW PP	SS KK CC U M E Q W II OO
DD	EE FF GG HH II JJ KK LL MM NN	W P I YY RR KK DD XX QQ JJ	LL DD V N F X JJ PP VV EE
EE	FF GG HH II JJ KK LL MM NN OO	X Q J ZZ SS LL EE YY RR KK	EE W O G A KK QQ WW X DD
FF	GG HH II JJ KK LL MM NN OO PP	Y R K D TT MM FF UU NN GG	VV NN FF GG MM H N T Z Y
GG	HH II JJ KK LL MM NN OO PP QQ	Z S L E UU NN GG TT MM FF	WW OO GG Y FF I O U AA MM
HH	II JJ KK LL MM NN OO PP QQ RR	AA T M F A VV OO HH UU NN	XX PP HH Z R P V BB NN TT
II	JJ KK LL MM NN OO PP QQ RR SS	BB U N G B WW PP II VV OO	YY QQ II AA S K W CC OO UU
JJ	KK LL MM NN OO PP QQ RR SS TT	CC V O H C XX QQ JJ WW PP	ZZ RR JJ BB T L D DD PP VV
KK	LL MM NN OO PP QQ RR SS TT UU	DD W P I YY RR KK XX QQ JJ	SS KK CC U M E RR EE QQ WW
LL	MM NN OO PP QQ RR SS TT UU VV	EE X Q J ZZ SS LL YY RR KK	LL DD V N F RR XX EE KK QQ
MM	NN OO PP QQ RR SS TT UU VV WW	FF Y R K D TT MM UU NN GG	UU MM NN TT FF I O U AA GG
NN	OO PP QQ RR SS TT UU VV WW XX	GG Z S L E UU NN TT MM FF	VV NN FF MM J P V BB HH TT
OO	PP QQ RR SS TT UU VV WW XX YY	HH AA T M F A VV OO UU NN	WW OO GG Y VV Q W CC II UU
PP	QQ RR SS TT UU VV WW XX YY ZZ	II BB U N G B WW PP VV OO	XX PP HH Z R OO X DD JJ VV
QQ	RR SS TT UU VV WW XX YY ZZ A	JJ CC V O H C XX QQ WW PP	YY QQ II AA S K EE KK WW XX
RR	SS TT UU VV WW XX YY ZZ A B	KK DD W P I YY RR XX QQ JJ	ZZ RR JJ BB T L D LL XX YY
SS	TT UU VV WW XX YY ZZ A B C	LL EE X Q J ZZ SS YY RR KK	SS KK CC U M E LL RR XX YY
TT	UU VV WW XX YY ZZ A B C D	MM FF Y R K D TT UU NN GG	J P V BB HH NN TT FF MM UU
UU	VV WW XX YY ZZ A B C D E	NN GG Z S L E UU TT MM FF	UU MM VV NN TT Q W CC II OO
VV	WW XX YY ZZ A B C D E F	OO HH AA T M F A VV UU NN	VV NN FF WW OO UU X DD JJ PP
WW	XX YY ZZ A B C D E F G	PP II BB U N G B WW VV OO	WW OO GG Y JJ PP VV EE KK QQ
XX	YY ZZ A B C D E F G H	XX QQ JJ CC V O H C WW PP	LL RR XX YY QQ WW PP HH Z R
YY	ZZ A B C D E F G H I	RR KK DD W P I YY XX QQ JJ	YY QQ II AA S K SS LL RR XX
ZZ	A B C D E F G H I J	ZZ SS LL EE X Q J YY RR KK	SS YY ZZ RR JJ BB T L D XX

EXCHANGE CHART

ORIGINAL NUMBER	ONE-DIGIT NUMBER	TWO-DIGIT NUMBER	THREE-DIGIT NUMBER	FOUR-DIGIT NUMBER
1	7	35	683	7151
2	1	42	372	8544
3	9	98	997	1989
4	4	48	692	8896
5	1	35	780	4225
6	6	98	994	8016
7	8	86	471	1409
8	6	92	408	6144
9	1	91	991	9991
10	1	50	830	1510
11	5	31	146	6992
12	6	92	988	3956
13	3	16	999	1412
14	2	78	584	7830
15	1	95	985	5040
16	4	68	648	3792
17	4	18	242	6806
18	2	82	982	9982
19	3	65	977	5869
20	1	20	720	5440
21	3	86	979	6923
22	2	64	306	3928
23	4	21	388	1435
24	4	92	976	2064
25	1	50	825	7175
26	2	24	176	7468

EXCHANGE CHART
(continued)

ORIGINAL NUMBER	ONE-DIGIT NUMBER	TWO-DIGIT NUMBER	THREE-DIGIT NUMBER	FOUR-DIGIT NUMBER
27	3	73	973	9973
28	6	80	124	1228
29	5	19	394	3888
30	1	80	970	9890
31	1	22	613	6444
32	6	64	192	5040
33	8	89	967	9088
34	6	32	102	1558
35	1	40	910	8130
36	4	64	964	9964
37	9	95	271	4587
38	1	98	168	2336
39	7	74	961	2857
40	1	80	920	8960
41	8	17	996	8645
42	2	86	958	6112
43	2	14	179	3941
44	8	56	744	8792
45	5	55	955	9955
46	2	10	418	8946
47	5	87	742	1784
48	4	68	952	5824
49	9	38	227	1476
50	1	50	800	2250
51	6	83	949	3136
52	8	96	356	7324